W9-COU-728

550

The Center Counter

John Grefe
International Master

and

Jeremy Silman
Senior Master

1983

Coraopolis, Pennsylvania

Chess Enterprises, Inc.

© Copyright 1983 by Chess Enterprises, Inc.

ISBN 0-931462-22-3

Editor: B. G. Dudley

Cover Design: E. F. Witalis, Jr.
                Witalis Burke Associates, Inc.
                Pittsburgh, PA

Preface

Although the Center Counter is almost five hundred years old, the first known recorded instance of the defense being the game Castellvi-Vinoles in 1485, it remains a theoretical enigma. Most modern theorists treat it with disdain, considering surprise it's chief virtue. Consequently it's appearance in grandmaster chess (the trendsetter of opening fashion) has always been sporadic. Sooner or later, such a neglected opening was bound to attract the attention of Danish Grandmaster Bent Larsen, an enterprising player constantly on the lookout for fresh opening ideas, or old ones that can be given a new twist.

At the Montreal 'Tournament of Stars' in 1979, Larsen ventured the Center Counter against two world champions! Although he was slaughtered by ex-champion Spassky after misplaying the opening, Larsen scored a stunning victory over Karpov, prompting other grandmasters to try the Center Counter. Then in 1982 Larsen had the temerity to play it against Karpov for a second time, suggesting that the Dane might even consider it to be sound.

So if you are looking for an opening that leads to lively tactics, has good surprise value, offers plenty of scope for experimentation and creativity (and may even be sound!) try the Center Counter. A further point in Black's favor is that White has no good way to sidestep the opening after 1 e4 d5. This means he must meet you on your own ground, and eliminates the necessity of learning numerous alternative lines.

Lest the foregoing create the wrong impression, we hasten to add that objectivity is the keynote of this book — the authors are not biased in favor of either side. You'll find a complete exposition of the basic strategies for both players, all the latest nuances, a review of the most important older lines, and a hearty selection of illustrative games.

In an effort to avoid just copying known theory, the authors have offered a large selection of new ideas and moves, which should make this book indespensible to the player who opens 1 e4, or to anyone considering the Center Counter for the Black side.

International Master John Grefe
Senior Master Jeremy Silman
California, 1982

Dedicated to Joyce & Barney Green for their great kindness to me. And to the little Beast (Sakmo, Sarah), magickal huntress of the wild Corrine.

OM NAMAh Shivaya

"Kneel to your own self. Honor and Worship your own Being. Meditate on your own Self. God dwells within you as you."

[Swami Muktananda]

"My adepts stand upright; their head above the heavens, their feet below the hells."

[Aiwass thru A. Crowley.]

Introduction

Black's basic idea in the Center Counter (also called the Scandinavian Defense) is to develop his pieces freely, quickly, and actively through an exchange of central pawns. The attractiveness of this idea can easily be seen when we compare the Center Counter with the other king pawn openings in which Black challenges White's king pawn with his queen pawn — the French Defense (1 e4 e6 2 d4 d5) and the Caro-Kann (1 e4 c6 2 d4 d5). In these openings, Black advances ...d5 only when he can recapture on that square with a pawn. That way he can maintain a pawn foothold in the center, and, if White exchanges, quickly equalize because of the symmetrical (or nearly symmetrical) central pawn position.

White rarely exchanges on d5 in the French, however, and Black often suffers from a cramped game, though he is not devoid of counterplay against White's pawn center. In the Caro-Kann, Black has nothing better than 3 Nc3, and finds himself with a passive, albeit solid, position. (Caro-Kann and Center Counter pawn structures are often identical.) A further drawback of the Caro-Kann is that the now superfluous move ...c6 (after 3 Nc3 dxe4) robs Black's queen knight of it's best square.

In the Center Counter, Black sidesteps the problems mentioned above but must nevertheless surmount certain obstacles before he can equalize. His main difficulties are backward development and a spatial inferiority in the center. The former results when White harrasses the piece that captures on d5 (the queen or knight) with natural developing moves. The latter is due to the fact that White can establish his queen pawn on the fourth rank while Black cannot easily challenge it with either his king pawn or queen bishop pawn. On the other hand, White's queen pawn sometimes becomes the target of a rapid counterattack. Many White players also fatally overextend their positions with premature attacks designed to refute a supposedly inferior opening.

The moves 1 e4 d5 introduce the Center Counter. After 2 exd5 Black plays either 2...Qxd5 or 2...Nf6. The former is covered in Part One of this book, the latter in Part Two. (After 2...Nf6 3 c4 c6 4 d4 cxd5 5 Nc3 the game transposes into the Panov-Botvinnik attack in the Caro-Kann; which is not covered in this book).

The bulk of Part One was done by John Grefe, Part Two by Jeremy Silman.

Summary and Conclusions

Black's ideal set-up involves ...Nc6, ...Bg4, and ...0-0-0, rapidly completing his development and putting pressure on White's queen pawn. The practical difficulties in achieving this formation, however, are nearly impossible to overcome.

In the 3...Qa5 lines, ...Nc6 rules out the queen's natural escape route with ...c6, and invites Bb5. This further cramps the queen and threatens to devastate Black's queenside pawn formation. If Black has to play ...bxc6 the pawns will be very weak in the ending, while in the middlegame they offer poor shelter for Black's king. Only in some unusual lines, as in Menas — Powell of Chapter Five, can Black allow the doubling of his pawns. In some lines ...Nc6 may run afoul of an early d4-d5 push.

...Bg4 is most often answered by h3. More experience is needed in the ...Bxf3 lines (Chapter Five, A), but it is hard to believe that surrendering the two bishops and crouching behind his pawns at e6 and c6 will prove healthy for Black. The relatively unanalyzed nature of the line, however, may appeal to adventurous types.

Nowadays the main line in the whole 3...Qa5 complex is B2b. of Chapter Five. Here again more practical experience is required, but the bulk of the material clearly favors White. The aggressive potential of his advanced kingside pawns outweighs their inherent weakness, and the danger to Black's queen bishop is a constant source of worry.

Chapter Four, sections B2a1. and B2b. represent Black's best opportunities to get a decent game without having to rely exclusively on tactical inventiveness. B2a2. has been very popular of late but has scored very well for White.

A well prepared White player would do best to enter the main lines, since the offbeat approaches of which B in Chapter Four is White's most potent, give Black great opportunities for a satisfactory game.

3...Qd8, on the whole, is poor for Black. Familiarity with the middlegames typical of the Parma — Germek line from game # 22 may compensate for the risks involved, especially if Black feels his opponent is poorly prepared. There are also the experimental ideas 5...Bf5 and 5...Bg4 mentioned in A of Chapter Six.

3...Qd6 is still in the embryonic stage, making it a perfect surprise weapon. The queen is more actively placed than on d8, but also more exposed.

In fact, the entire 2...Qxd5 complex is still a good surprise weapon offering wide scope for the inventive tactician. Black must never lose sight of the fact that he is taking a calculated risk in the great majority of variations.

The variations arising from 2...Nf6 (Part Two) often lead to play which is very similar to Alekhine's Defense, with White having an imposing center and Black trying to strike it down.

White should avoid Chapter One and the resulting Black pawn sacrifice as it gives Black too great of an initiative. Results tend to heavily favor Black.

The once popular lines from Chapter Two lead to very tense situations, but Black is never at a loss for counterplay and can be very happy if White enters the variation.

Chapter Three, B3., can be considered the critical chapter for the whole of Part Two. White, with his central advantage and spatial edge, should end up with a superior game. In particular, the controversial variation from Chapter Three, B3b1., seems to offer White great chances in several ways . . . the move 7 Bg5! being especially interesting. If this is too sharp for White's tastes, the quieter 6 Be2 (instead of 6 c5) from B3b2. also offers White bright prospects.

In conclusion, if one has to choose between 2...Qxd5 and 2...Nf6, the wiser choice might very well be 2...Qxd5; for the simple reason that it is the less analyzed and least explored of the two.

Part 2, P. 50

Part One

Chapter One

1 e4   d5

Diagram 1   After 1...d5

A. 2 Nf3?! ; B. 2 e5 ; C. Nc3 ; D. 2 exd5.

A.

2 Nf3?!

This gambit line gives Black a great game after **2...dxe4 3 Ng5 Bf5 4 Bc4 e6 5 Nc3 Nf6 6 Qe2 Nc6.**

B.

2 e5

Black has a number of ways to deal with this unusual line, e.g., even 2...e6, 2...c6, or 2...Nc6 are playable. One of the strongest moves is 2...Bf5, probably leading to a type of French Defense in which Black has solved the problem of his queen bishop. 2...c5 seems to be the most natural move. After 3 c3, 3...d4 is the most challenging response (usually seen from a Sicilian move order via: 1 e4 c5 2 c3 d5 3 e5 d4 etc.). 2...d4 is a tit-for-tat strategy, not always advisable for Black. Many of the lines mentioned here have the virtue of being completely unexplored, though of course many transpositions to well-known lines are also possible.

C.

2 Nc3

Once again Black has a wide selection of moves at his disposal. 2...Nf6 3 e5 Nfd7 4 d4 e6 leads to the French Defense, while 3...d4 or 3...Nfd7 4 Nxd5 belongs to Alekhine's Defense. 3 exd5 Nxd5 can be found in Part Two of this work.

Black's simplest course to equality is 2...dxe4 3 Nxe4 Nf6 (or 3...e5) 4 Nxf6+ gxf6. 2...d4 leads to a type of King's Indian Reversed → see game 1.

D.

2 exd5

D1.

2 ....   c6?

2...c6? is an unsound gambit best disposed of by **3 dxc6 Nxc6 4 Nf3 e5 5 Bb5.**

D2.

2	e6?

Equally unpromising for Black. After **3 dxe6 Bxe6 4 d4 Nc6 5 Nf3** Black has nothing to show for his pawn.

Chapter Two

1 e4	d5
2 exd5	Qxd5

Diagram 2   After 2...Qxd5

A. 3 Nf3 ; B. 3 d4.

A.

3 Nf3

A1. 3...e5?! ; A2. 3...Bg4.

By allowing the queen to remain centralized for the moment, White hopes to tempt his opponent into over-reaching himself.

A1.

3	e5?!
4 Nc3	Qe6

4...Qa5 transposes to Chapter Four, A.

5 Be2

Blazes new trails, and will probably favor White after an eventual d4. (It hardly seems likely that Black can get away with 5...c5!?).

A2.

3	Bg4
4 Be2	

4 Nc3 Qa5 probably transposes to lines analysed later. 4...Qd7 will probably prove inferior after 5 h3 Bh5 6 g4 Bg6 7 d4, intending a quick Ne5.

If Black doesn't mind simplifying, then he can try 4...Qe6† 5 Qe2 Qxe2† 6 Bxe2 Nc6 for easy equality, though White may try to complicate with 5 Be2 Bxf3 6 gxf3 etc. To be avoided is 4...Bxf3? 5 Nxd5 Bxd1 6 Nxc7† Kd8

7 Nxa8 Bxc2 8 d3! +−.

4	Nc6

Once again the twofold advance of the king pawn seems ill-advised. After 4...e5?! 5 Nc3 Qa5 6 0-0 Nc6 for example, White has the strong 7 Nxe5!

5 Nc3	Qa5
6 h3	Bh5
7 d4	0-0-0
8 Be3	e5
9 Nxe5	Bxe2
10 Qxe2	Nxe5
11 dxe5	Qxe5 =

But not 11...Ba3?! 12 Qb5! Qxb5 13 Nxb5 Bxb2 14 Rb1 Bxe5 15 Nxa7†, etc.

B.

3 d4

B1. 3...e5; B2. 3...Nc6.

B1.

3	e5

Here this equalizes, though there's little practical experience with the line. Now White has B1a. 4 dxe5; B1b. 4 Nf3; B1c. 4 Nc3.

B1a.

4 dxe5	Qxe5†

4...Qxd1†!?

5 Be2	Bg4

This is fine for Black.

B1b.

4 Nf3	Bg4!

This likewise gives Black a comfortable game.

B1c.

4 Nc3	Qxd4
5 Qxd4	exd4
6 Nb5	Na6

6...Bb4† 7 Bd2 Bxd2† 8 Kxd2 Na6 9 Re1† is a bit awkward for Black.

7 Nxd4	Nb4! =

B2.

3	Nc6

This might be preferred by those seeking a more complicated game than offered by the above lines.

B2a. 4 Nf3 e5?! ; B2b. 4 Nf3 Bg4.

B2a.

4 Nf3	e5?!

10

5 Nc3	

5 dxe5 is akin to the idea 4...Qxd1† mentioned in B1a.

5	Bb4
6 Bd2	Bxc3
7 Bxc3	e4
8 Ne5	Nxe5
9 dxe5	Ne7
10 Qh5	

brought White a clear plus in Shabahov-Lazarichev, Astrakhan 1978.

B2b.

4 Nf3	Bg4

B2b1. 5 Be2 ; B2b2. 5 Nc3.

B2b1.

5 Be2	0-0-0
6 Nc3	Qa5
7 Be3	

This is similar to A.2. It can also transpose to game # 16 after 7...Nf6 8 Nd2.

B2b2.

5 Nc3	Qa5

5...Bxf3? 6 Nxd5; 5...Qh5!?

This main line position can arise after 1 e4 d5 2 exd5 Qxd5 3 Nc3 Qa5 4 Nf3 Nc6 5 d4 Bg4, or via the Nimzovitch Defense move order 1 e4 Nc6 2 Nf3 d5 3 exd5 Qxd5 4 Nc3 Qa5 5 d4 Bg4, which was the actual order of the game in B2b2a.

Diagram 3

After 5...Qa5

B2b21. 6 h3; B2b2b. 6 d5; B2b2c. 6 Bb5; B2b2d. 6 Be2.

B2b2a.

6 h3	Bxf3

6...Bh5 may also be playable. This whole section from here on is largely unexplored, and since it is only a sub-variation, the analysis is limited to a consideration of the major possibilities.

7	Qxf3	0-0-0
8	Qxf7	e5!
9	d5	Nd4

This led to a stunning victory for Black in game # 2 (Suetin — Knaak, 1982).

B2b2b.

6	d5

This may be favorable to White, e.g.:

6	....	0-0-0
7	Bd2	Ne5

7...Nb4!?

8	Be2	Bxf3
9	Bxf3	Nf6

9...Nc4!?

10	Qe2	Nxf3†
11	Qxf3	

and this line is good for White since 11...e6? 12 dxe6 Re8 fails to 12 Ne2!

B2b2c.

6	Bb5	0-0-0
7	Bxc6	bxc6
8	h3	Bh5
9	g4	Bg6
10	Bd2	

10 Ne5!?

10	....	Nf6
11	Ne5	Qa6
12	Qf3	

White stands better.

B2b2d.

6	Be2	0-0-0
7	Be3	e5

This leads back to B2b1.

Perhaps East Germany's brilliant Grandmaster Rainer Knaak will add to our knowledge of the above lines in the near future.

Chapter Three

1	e4	d5
2	exd5	Qxd5
3	Nc3	Qa5

Diagram 4   After 3...Qa5

A. 4 Nf3; B. 4 Bc4.

A.

4 Nf3

Once again White hopes to lure his opponent into a premature central advance. 4 Nf3 e5?! 5 d4 for example transposes into A. of Chapter Four, which favors White.

Besides the two moves given above (4 Nf3 and 4 Bc4), other fourth moves are: i. 4 b3. Black secures equality with 4...e5 5 Bb2 Ba3! ii. 4 Nge2 is new. One possible continuation is 4...Nf6 5 d4 Nc6 6 Ng3 h5. iii. 4 g3 is also experimental, but holds out more promise of an advantage than 4 b3 or 4 Nge2. One scenario: 4...e5 5 Bg2 Nf6 6 Nf3 (6 Nge2!?) 6...Nc6 7 0-0 Be7 8 d4 exd4 9 Nxd4 Nxd4 10 Qxd4 0-0. iv. 4 b4(?) has long been considered dubious because of the game Thomas — du Mont, Tunbridge Wells, 1912: 4...Qxb4 5 Rb1 Qd6 6 Nf3 Nf6 7 d4 a6! 8 Bc4 e6 9 0-0 Be7 10 Re1 b5 11 Bb3 Bb7 12 Bg5 Nbd7 ∓.

A1. 4...g6; A2. 4...c5; A3. 4...Nf6; A4. 4...Bg4(?); A5. 4...Nc6.

A1.

4 ....   g6

This worked well in L. Paulsen — Blackburne, 1873 after:

5	Bc4	Bg7
6	0-0	Nc6
7	d3	Nh6
8	Bd2	Qh5
9	Nd5	Bg4!
10	Nf4	Qf5
11	h3	Bxf3

13

12	Qxf3	0-0-0
13	Bd5	Nd4!
14	Qe4	e5 =

The antidote may be 5 d4 Bg7 6 Bf4 intending 7 Be5.

A2.

| 4 | .... | c5 |

This move had a successful debut in Burkhard — Powell, California 1982, which ran:

5	Bb5†	Bd7
6	Bxd7†	Nxd7
7	0-0	Ngf6
8	d4	cxd4
9	Qxd4	e6
10	Bf4	Bc5 =

A3.

| 4 | .... | Nf6 |

5 d4 transposes to main lines analysed further on.

| 5 | Bc4 | Bg4?! |

See B4a. for other fifth moves.

| 6 | h3! | Bh5 |

6...Qh5 7 Be2 ±

7	Qe2!	Nbd7
8	g4	Bg6
9	b4!?	

and this sequence leads to game # 3.

A4.

| 4 | .... | Bg4?! |

Besides 5 h3 Bh5 6 Bc4 with play similar to A3., White can introduce most likely favorable complications by 5 b4!?.

A5.

4	....	Nc6
5	Bb5	Bd7
6	0-0	

6 d4 a6!? is uncharted terrain.

| 6 | .... | e6 |
| 7 | d4 | |

led to an advantage for White in Reti — Rubenstein, 1922, after:

7	....	Bb4
8	Qd3	Bxc3
9	bxc3	a6
10	Bc4	Nge7
11	Rb1	Rb8

12 Ng5!

6...a6!?, however, may give Black a reasonable game. For 5 Bc4 see B3c. or B4a. 5 d4 Bg4 leads to B2b2. in Chapter Two. 4...c6 and 4...Bf5 will likely revert to main lines in a few moves.

B.
4 Bc4

Diagram 5   After 4 Bc4

B1. 4...c5; B2. 4...e5; B3. 4...Nc6; B4. 4...Nf6.

Here 4...g6? is weak. Black lands in serious trouble after 5 Qf3! Nf6 6 Nd5!. 4...c6 probably transposes to other lines, but 4...Bf5?! involves Black in the complications of 5 Qf3 Nc6 6 Bb5 or 5...c6 6 b4.

B1.
4	c5

This might be playable, e.g., the primitive attack 5 Qh5 e6 6 Ne4 Nc6 7 Nf3 is beaten back after 7...Be7, intending 8...g6.

Perhaps 5 b3!?.

B2.
4	e5

Probably too ambitious. White quickly usurped the initiative in Klovan — Pavlenko, USSR 1973:

5 Nf3	Bd6
6 d4	exd4
7 Qxd4	Nf6
8 Qe3†	

See B3b1. below.

B3.
4	Nc6

B3a. 5 d3; B3b. 5 d4; B3c. 5 Nf3.

B3a.
5 d3	Bd7
6 Bd2	Qf5

7	Nge2	Nf6
8	Ng3	Qg4
9	f3	Qh4

A double-edged position.

B3b.

5	d4

B3b1. 5...e5; B3b2. 5...Bf5; B3b3. 5...g6.

B3b1.

5	....	e5

Untested. It can also arise via other move orders. Klovan — Pavlenko in B2, for instance, went 4 Nf3 e5 5 Bc4. Of course, in this sequence 5...Nc6 6 d3, intending 7 Bd2, might prove uncomfortable to Black.

B3b2.

5	....	Bf5!?

New and untried.

B3b3.

5	....	g6!?

Also an innovation.

B3c.

5	Nf3	Bg4

Probably satisfactory for Black.

B4.

4	....	Nf6

B4a. 5 Nf3; B4b. 5 d4.

B4a.

5	Nf3	Bg4?!

Transposes to A3. 5...c6 or 5...Bf5 will convert to the main lines after 6 d4. For 5...Nc6 6 d4 Bg4 see game # 4 (Note 1).

B4b.

5	d4

Black equalized without any trouble in Shaw — Purdy, Sydney 1979, after 5 d3 c6 6 Bd2 Qb6 7 Rb1 Bg4.

Most likely transposing are 6...c6 or 5...Bf5, though White might venture 6 Nge2!?.

B4b1. 5...Bg4?!; B4b2. 5...Nc6?!

B4b1.

5	....	Bg4?!

This continuation can be found in game # 4.

B4b2.

5	....	Nc6?!
6	d5	

For 6 Nf3 Bg4 see game # 4. Mieses once analysed 6 Nge2 Be6, but Pachman claims it favors White after 7 Bxe6 fxe6 8 Bf4 0-0-0 9 Qc1.

	6	Ne5
	7 Bb3	c6
	8 Qe2	Ned7
	9 Bd2	cxd5
	10 Nxd5	Qd8
	11 Nxf6†!	Nxf6

11...gxf6 12 Qh5.

12 0-0-0

Black is saddled with an awkward defensive task.

Chapter Four

	1 e4	d5
	2 exd5	Qxd5
	3 Nc3	Qa5
	4 d4	

Diagram 6

After 4 d4

A. 4...e5?!; B. 4...Nf6 5 Nf3.

As usual there are a number of transpositional possibilities such as 4...c6 or 4...Bf5. 4...Nc6?! and 4...g6?! both appear dubious. Line 'A.' is known as Anderssen's variation. It's main virtue appears to be historical interest since the early opening of the position is bound to favor White.

A.

4 .... e5?!

A1. 5 dxe5; A2. 5 Nf3!

A1.

5 dxe5

May also favor White, though it's more obscure than A2. E.g.:

5 .... Nc6

5...Bb4 6 Bd2 Bf5 is untested, but 6...Nc6 7 a3! Nd4 8 Nge2 Bg4 9 f3

Bxf3 10 axb4! should be avoided by Black.

6	Nf3		Bb4

6...Bd7!?; 6...Bg4!?.

7	Bd2		Bg4
8	Bb5		Nge7
9	a3		Bxf3
10	gxf3		Bxc3
11	Bxc6†		Nxc6
12	Bxc3		Qa4
13	Rg1!?, etc.		

13 Qd2 Rd8 14 Qg5 0-0 15 e6 Nd4 gives White nothing.

A2.

5	Nf3!

A2a. 5...Bb4; A2b. 5...Bg4; A2c. 5...exd4.

A2a.

5	....		Bb4
6	Bd2		Bg4

6...exd4 7 Qe2† Ne7 8 Nxd4 0-0 9 a3.

7	a3

For 7 Be2 see game #5.

7	....		Bd6

7...Bxf3 8 axb4.

8	Bc4	±	

If 8...exd4, 9 Qe2†.

A2b.

5	....		Bg4
6	h3		exd4

6...Bh5 7 g4! exd4 8 Qxd4 Nc6 9 Bb5 was very unpleasant for Black in Suetin — Dankevich, 1960.

7	Qxd4		Bxf3
8	Qe3† etc.		

A2c.

5	....		exd4
6	Nxd4		Bb4
7	Bd2		Qe5†
8	Qe2		Qxe2†
9	Bxe2		c6
10	Ne4!		Bxd2†
11	Kxd2	+—	

Sergeant — Mieses, London 1934.

4	....	**Nf6**
5 Nf3		

Only this knight move or 5 Bc4, which transposes either to the previous chapter or to B2 below, hold out much chance for a serious opening advantage. 5 Bd3; 5 Be2; 5 Nge2 and 5 g3 have rarely, if ever, appeared in master chess. For the slightly more popular 5 Bd2 see game #6.

B1. 5...Nc6?!; B2. 5...c6.

B1.

5	....	**Nc6?!**

See game #7.

B2.

5	....	**c6**

5...Bf5 generally amounts to a mere transposition of moves after 6 Ne5, 6 Bc4 or 6 Bd2, which Black usually answers with 6...c6. This would appear to make 5...Bf5 less accurate, for Black thus loses the options of answering 6 Ne5 with 6...Be6, and 6 Bc4 with 6...Bg4. In Dzuric — Larsen, Copenhagen 1979, the move order 5...Bf5 6 Bc4 (6 Bd3 e6 7 Bxf5 Qxf5 8 Ne5 h5 9 0-0 Nbd7 10 Qe2 a6 11 f4 Rd8 12 Rf3 Nb6 13 Rg3 Nbd5 soon led to an obscure situation in Barle — Larsen, Portoroz 1979 while 7 0-0 Nbd7 8 Bf4 c6 9 a3 Bxd3 10 Qxd3 Be7 11 Ne4 Nxe4 12 Qxe4 Nf6 13 Qe2 Qf5 also brought White very little in Radulov — Taulbut, Copenhagen 1981.) 6...Nbd7 7 Qe2 e6 8 Bd2 Bb4 9 a3 0-0 10 0-0 Bxc3 11 Bxc3 Qb6 only brought White a small plus, but 7 Bd2! c6 (7...e6 8 Nd5) 8 Qe2 e6 9 d5! would have transposed to game #11.

Diagram 7

After 5...c6

The advantage of 5...c6, a move Black must make sooner or later in order to give his queen an escape route, is that Black can answer 6 Bc4 with 6...Bg4 and avoid the lines in Chapter Five with 5...Bg4 6 h3. It is not clear, however, that this makes his prospects any brighter.

B2a. 6 Bc4; B2b. 6 Ne5; B2c. 6 Bd2.

B2a.
6 Bc4

6 Be2 is very passive. The best answer seems to be 6...Bf5! (For 6...Bg4 see Chapter Five.)

B2a1. 6...Bg4; B2a2. 6...Bf5.

6...e6? condemns Black to passivity. Benko — Lyons, USA 1966 continued 7 0-0 Be7 8 Re1 0-0 9 Bg5 Nbd7 10 Ne4 Re8 11 Ng3 Qc7 12 Qe2 Nb6 13 Bd3 Nbd5 14 Ne5 with a sharp kingside attack in the air.

B2a1.

6	....	**Bg4**	
7	**h3**	**Bh5**	

7...Qh5? 8 Be2! e6 9 0-0 ± ; for 7...Bxf3 see Chapter Five, A.

8 Qe2

8 g4 Bg6 9 Ne5 Nbd7 10 Nxg6 hxg6 11 Qe2 e6 12 Bd2 Bb4 13 0-0-0 Nd5 = , Lau — N. Fries Nielsen, Clare Benedict 1979.

8	....	**e6**

8...Nbd7 9 Bd2 Bxf3 10 Qxf3 Qb6 11 0-0-0 Qxd4? 12 Bxf7†! Kxf7 13 Be3 Ne5 14 Qg3 Qd6 15 Rxd6 +— Mestel — Lein, Hastings 1980/81.

9	**Bd2**	**Qd8?**

9...Bb4!?

10	**g4**	**Bg6**
11	**0-0-0**	**Nbd7**
12	**Ne5**	

With a powerful White initiative in Matera — Willis, USA 1969.

B2a2.

6	....	**Bf5**
7	**Bd2**	**e6**

7...Nbd7? 8 Qe2 e6 9 d5! is game # 11. For 7...Qc7 8 0-0 see game # 10.

8	**Qe2**	**Bb4**

8...Bxc2? 9 d5!

9 Ne5

9 0-0-0 Nd5 is game # 13; 9 a3 Bg4 is game # 14.

9	....	**Nbd7**
10	**0-0-0**	

This variation brought White a substantial plus in game # 15.

B2b.

6	**Ne5**	**Bf5**

Two alternatives to 6...Bf5, both of which deserve closer scrutiny, are:
6...Be6 7 Nc4 Bxc4 8 Bxc4 e6 9 Bd2 Qc7 10 Qf3 Nbd7 11 0-0-0 0-0-0 12 Bg5 Be7 with a rock-solid position for Black in Sloan — Popel, USA 1973; and 6...Nbd7!? 7 Nc4 Qd8 intending a quick Nb6 followed by ...Bf5. Perhaps 7 f4!?;

7 Bc4

7 g4!? might suit the hyper-aggressive. Black of course has a number of responses, an interesting tactical possibility being 7...Be6 8 Bc4? Nxg4! — + . Also leading to nothing for White was 8 Nc4 Qc7 9 Ne3 Nbd7 10 g5 Nd5 11 Ncxd5 Bxd5 12 Nxd5 cxd5 13 c3 e6 = , Matanovic — Janicijevski, Vrsac 1979; Larsen himself in the Encyclopedia, recommends 7 f4!. On occasion, 7 Bd3 has also been played: 7...Bxd3 8 Qxd3 e6 9 0-0 (9 Bd2 Nbd7 10 Qe2 Be7 11 0-0-0 Nxe5 12 dxe5 Nd7 13 f4 ± , Marjanovic — Janicijevski, Vrsac 1979) 9...Nbd7 10 Nxd7 Kxd7!? 11 Ne4 Nxe4 12 Qxe4 Qd5 13 Qe2 brought White a small edge in Medina — Larsen, Las Palmas 1974; while 8... Nbd7 9 f4 Nxe5?! 10 fxe5 Nd5 11 0-0 led to a rapid debacle for Black in the early days of this defense in the game Wolf — Mieses, Dusseldorf 1908.

| 7 .... | e6 |

7...Bg6!?

8 g4

8 0-0 Nbd7 9 Qe2 Bb4 10 Nxd7 Nxd7 11 Ne4 Bxe4 12 Qxe4 Bd2 13 c3 Bxc1 14 Rxc1 0-0 15 Rfe1 brought White a small but enduring pull in Fedorowica — Ciric, England 1981; 8...Bb4 9 Ne2 Nbd7 12 Nxd7 Nxd7 13 Bf4 0-0 12 c3 Be7 13 Re1 Rfd8 14 Ng3 Bg6 15 Qf3 ± exemplifies another approach for White, as played in Sokolov — K. Hansen, Groningen 1981-82.

| 8 .... | Bg6 |

8...Be4!?

9 h4	Nbd7
10 Nxd7	Nxd7
11 h5	Be4
12 Rh3	Bd5
13 Qe2	Bb4
14 Bd2	Bxc4
15 Qxc4	Nb6
16 Qd3	

and now **16...Rd8** would have led to an unclear position, instead of 16... Nd5?! 17 Rf3 h6 18 g3 Bxc3 19 bxc3 favoring White in Shamkovich — Sveshnikov, USSR 1971.

B2c.
6 Bd2

This brought White a smashing success in Klovan — Schvedchikov, Odessa 1981, after:

| 6 .... | Qb6 |

6...Qc7 7 Bc4 e6? see game # 8.

Perhaps safest for Black is the transposition to B2a2 by 6...Bf5 7 Bc4 e6 8 Qe2 though this also has been shown to be good for White.

| 7 Bc4 | Qxb2 |

8 d5! Nbd7 9 0-0 Nb6 10 dxc6! bxc6 11 Bb3 Qa3 12 Ne5 e6 13 Qf3, etc.

Chapter Five

1 e4	d5
2 exd5	Qxd5
3 Nc3	Qa5
4 d4	Nf6
5 Nf3	Bg4

Diagram 8  After 5...Bg4

The diagrammed position is currently regarded as the starting point of the main lines in the 3...Qa5 variation. Besides 6 h3, White can also play 6 Be2, which can be found in game # 16; or the experimental 6 Bd2, as in Menas — Powell, California 1982, which continued 6...Nc6 (for 6...c6 see game # 12) 7 Bb5 0-0-0 8 Bxc6 bxc6 9 h3 with complications (9...Qh5!?).

A. 6 h3 Bxf3 7 Qxf3 c6; B. 6 h3 Bh5 7 g4 Bg6 8 Ne5.

A.

6 h3	Bxf3
7 Qxf3	c6
8 Bd2	Nbd7
9 0-0-0	e6

9...0-0-0 10 Bc4 e6 11 Ne4 Qa4 12 Bb3 Qxd4 13 Ng5 Ne5 14 Qe2 Ba3 15 c3 Nd3† 16 Kc2 Qxf2 17 Qxf2 Nxf2 18 Nxf7 Bd6 19 Bg5 Nxd1 20 Rxd1 Be7 21 Bxe6† Kc7 22 Bf4† Kb6 23 Be3† Kc7 24 Nxh8 led to a very favorable endgame for White in Gufeld — Mordintyev, USSR 1980.

10 Bc4	Qc7
11 Rhe1	0-0-0
12 Bb3	Bd6
13 Kb1	Kb8
14 g4	h6
15 h4	Rhf8

This is recommended by Grandmaster Larry Evans as Black's best way of handling the 3...Qa5 variation. He regards the position after Black's fifteenth as unclear, but earlier White could have played more actively, e.g., 11 g4 hinders Black's plan of castling long. If 11...Nb6 12 Bb3 0-0-0 13 g5 Nfd5 14 Ne4 is to White's advantage. Practical examples with 6...Bxf3 are lacking.

B.

6 h3	Bh5
7 g4	

For 7 Bd2 see game # 17.

7	Bg6
8 Ne5	

B1. 8...c6; B2. 8...e6.

B1.

8	c6

8...Nbd7? 9 Nc4 Qa6 10 Bf4 Qe6† 11 Ne3 etc., or 8...Ne4? 9 Qf3 Nd6 (9...Nxc3 10 bxc3 c6 11 Bc4 e6 12 h4) 10 Bd2 c6 11 h4!).

9 h4

9 Nc4 Qc7 10 Qf3 Bxc2 11 Bf4 Qd7 12 Rc1! (12 Qe2?! Bg6 13 Nd6† Kd8 is far from clear) 12...Bg6 13 d5! gives White an overwhelming initiative.

9	Nbd7

Both 9...Be4 10 Rg1 (or 10 Nc4 Qc7 11 Nxe4 Nxe4 12 Qf3 Nf6 13 Bf4 Qd7 14 g5) 10...Bd5 11 Nc4 Bxc4 12 Bxc4 e6 13 Bd2 Qb6 14 Qe2 Bb4 15 0-0-0 Nbd7 16 d5 cxd5 17 g5, Inkjov — Pantaleev, Sofia 1980; and 9...Ne4 10 Bd2 are extremely unappetizing for Black.

10 Nc4	Qc7
11 h5	Be4
12 Rh4!	

12 Nxe4 Nxe4 13 Qf3 is also good for White.

12	Bd5
13 g5	Bxc4
14 Bxc4	Nb6
15 Bb3	Nfd5
16 Nxd5	Nxd5
17 c4	

and Black was squashed in this 1962 game between Krashov — Bondar.

B2.

8	e6

(See Diagram 9 at top of next page)

8...e6 was first played in game # 18, Zuckerman — Shamkovich, Cleveland 1975. It gave the 3...Qa5 line a new lease on life which, however, may prove to be brief.

B2a. 9 Nc4; B2b. 9 Bg2 c6.

Diagram 9　　　　　　　　　　　　After 8...e6

B2a.

9 Nc4

See game # 18.

B2b.

9 Bg2　　　　c6

Other moves are weak: i. 9...Be4 10 Bxe4! (10 Nc4 Qb4 11 a3 Qxc4 12 Nxe4 Nxe4 13 Bxe4 ±) 10...Nxe4 11 Qf3 Nd6 12 Nxf7! (12 Bd2 f6! 13 Nd3 Nc6 ∞) 12...Nxf7 13 Qxb7 Qb6! (13...Bb4 14 Qxa8 Bxc3† 15 bxc3 Qxc3† 16 Ke2 + −) 14 Qxa8 c6 15 d5! + −; ii. 9...Qa6 10 h4 Bb4 11 h5 Be4 12 f3 Bd5 13 h6; iii. 9...Nd5 10 Bd1; iv. 9...Ne4 10 Nxg6 Nxc3 11 bxc3.

B2b1. 10 h4 ; B2b2. 10 0-0.

B2b1.

10 h4

See game # 19.

B2b2.

10 0-0

See game # 20.

Chapter Six

1 e4   d5
2 exd5   Qxd5
3 Nc3   Qd8
4 d4

Diagram 10   After 4 d4

A. 4...Nf6; B. 4...g6.

A.

4 ....   Nf6
5 Bc4

This move was Fischer's first choice; see game # 21. On 5 Nf3 (5 Be3 worked well for White in Tarrasch — Pillsbury, 1903 after 5...c6 6 Bd3 Bg4 7 Nge2 e6 8 Qd2 Bd6 9 Ng3 Qc7 10 h3! Bxg3 11 hxg3 Nxg4 12 fxg3 Qxg3† 13 Bf2 Qxg2 14 Be4) Black might try 5...Bf5. In comparison to Parma — Germek, given in the notes to game # 21, Black could save a tempo if he doesn't have to play ...c6.

For the adventurous there is 5...Bg4!?. On 6 h3 Bxf3 7 Qxf3 c6, some books recommend 8 Bf4 Qxd4 9 Nb5 (9 Rd1 Qb6 favors the pawn-snatcher). After 9...cxb5 10 Bxb5† Nbd7 11 0-0 Qd5! however, White has little to show for his piece. Boleslavsky says that 8 Bd2 Qxd4 9 0-0-0 (some sources even give 9 Nb5 here!) gives White a strong attack, but 9...Nbd7 again places the burden of proof on White.

B.

4 ....   g6

See game # 22.

1	e4	d5
2	exd5	Qxd5
3	Nc3	Qd6
4	d4	

Diagram 11   After 4 d4

4	....	Nf6

4...Nc6? 5 d5 Ne5 6 Bf4; 4...g6? 5 Nb5 etc.

A. 5 Bc4; B. 5 Bd3; C. 5 Bg5; D. 5 Nf3.

A.

5	Bc4	a6

White threatened an eventual Nb5.

6	Bb3	

6 Nge2!?

6	....	Nc6
7	Nge2	Bg4

7...Bf5!?

8	f3	Bh5

It's hard to understand this move; 8...Bf5!?.

9	Bf4	

9 d5!?

9	....	Qd7

9...e5!?

10	Qd2	e6
11	a3	0-0-0

With his bishop on f5 Black could play 11...Na5 12 Ba2 Qc6.

12	0-0-0	h6
13	Rhe1	g5
14	Be3	Bg7
15	Ng3	Bg6
16	d5!	

with advantage to White in Mährlein — Bigot, West Germany 1978. Obviously only the tip of the iceberg.

B.

5	Bd3	a6

5...Nc6!? 6 Nge2 e5!?.

6	Nge2	Nbd7
7	Bf4	Qc6
8	0-0	e6
9	Re1	Be7
10	Ng3	0-0
11	d5	Qb6
12	dxe6	fxe6
13	Bc4	Kh8

and now instead of entering the complications of 14 Rxe6 Qxb2 as in Baikov — Lazarichev, Moscow 1978, simply 14 Bb3 guarantees White a big edge.

C.

5	Bg5	c6

Now 5...a6 6 Qd2 Nc6 7 d5 is ±. The possibility of Bxf6 makes the White queen pawn a tower of strength on d5.

6	Bc4	Bg4
7	f3	Bf5
8	Nge2	Nbd7
9	Qd2	e6
10	0-0-0	Qc7
11	g4	Bg6
12	h4	b5
13	Bd3	

13 Bb3 h6 14 Bxf6 Nxf6 15 Nf4 Bh7 16 g5 Bd6 17 Nce2 Nd5 is okay for Black.

13	....	Qa5
14	Kb1	Be7
15	Bxf6	Nxf6
16	h5	Bxd3
17	Qxd3	

was advantageous for White in Jurcyska — Pytel, Poland 1976.

D.

5	Nf3	a6
6	Bc4	

For 6 Be3 see game # 23.

6	....	Bf5

6...Bg4!? 7 h3 Bh5.

7	0-0	Nc6
8	d5	Nb4?

8...Na5!

9	a3!	Nxc2
10	Nh4	Bg6!
11	Ra2	0-0-0
12	Bb3	

and White was winning in Winslow — Vickers, California 1981.

Illustrative Games, Part I

Game # 1

Casper — Mobius, East German Championship 1980

1	e4	d5
2	Nc3	

This position is also reached via the Saragossa Opening: 1 Nc3 d5 2 e4.

2	....	d4

Black was obviously in the mood for a complex struggle.

3	Nce2	e5
4	Ng3	

4 d3 is better because White maintains his options. He can play a quick f4, develop his king knight on 'f3', and increase his pressure on 'd4' after playing c2-c3, and fianchetto his king bishop. Now White only succeeds in developing his king bishop on its best square because of Black's careless play.

4	....	c5?!
5	Bc4	Nc6
6	N1e2	g6
7	0-0	Bg7
8	d3	Nge7
9	f4	exf4
10	Bxf4	0-0
11	Qd2	Be6
12	Bxe6	fxe6
13	Bh6	Qd6
14	Qg5	

Diagram 12   After 14 Qg5

Although Black has completed his development through a series of natural moves, he is hard-pressed to resist White's kingside initiative. The moral: even "harmless" variations become dangerous if they are met with sterotyped moves.

14	....	Bxh6
15	Qxh6	Ne5
16	Nf4	Ng4
17	Qg5	Ne3
18	e5	Qc6
19	Ne4	Rf7
20	Rf3	Raf8
21	Nf6†	Kh8
22	Rh3	Rg7
23	Nxh7	Rxh7
24	Qxe7	Resigns.

Game # 2
Suetin — Knaak, 1982

1	e4	Nc6
2	Nf3	d5
3	exd5	Qxd5
4	Nc3	Qa5
5	d4	Bg4

The position after Black's fifth move seems to be exactly what he's seeking from this variation. With three pieces already developed and bearing on White's center, Black is ready to castle long and play ...e5. Yet the strong 6 Bb5! seems to cast doubt on Black's ambitious designs. Black's shattered queenside will then prove a serious handicap.

6	h3?!	

Playing into Black's hands.

6	....	Bxf3
7	Qxf3	0-0-0
8	Qxf7	

White already has serious problems, e.g. 8 Be3 e5! 9 dxe5 Bb4.

8	....	e5!

So that if 9 dxe5 Bb4 10 Bd2 Qxe5†, etc.

9	d5	Nd4
10	Bg5	

10 Bd3 Nf6 would leave White having to try 11 d6 to extricate his queen.

10	....	Nf6
11	Bxf6	gxf6

(See diagram at top of next page)

Diagram 13   After 11...gxf6

12 Bd3

The only chance to put up a fight was 12 0-0-0 Bb4 13 Rd3! but not 13 Nb1 Qa4! 14 Bd3 Qxc2†! 15 Bxc2 Ne2 mate.

	12	Ba3!

Now White is lost.

13	0-0	Bxb2
14	Ne4	Bxa1
15	Rxa1	f5
16	Nf6	e4
17	Bf1	Rhf8
18	Qe7	Rxf6!
19	Qxf6	Qc3

Resigns.

Game # 3
Rohde — Seirawan, USA Junior Championship 1976

1	e4	d5
2	exd5	Qxd5
3	Nc3	Qa5
4	Nf3	Nf6
5	Bc4	Bg4?!
6	h3	Bh5
7	Qe2	Nbd7
8	g4	Bg6
9	b4	

(See diagram at top of next page)

Excessively violent. 9 d3! c6 10 Bd2 Qc7 11 0-0-0 0-0-0 (11...e6 12 Nh4 Be7 13 f4 Nd5 14 Ng2 Nb6 15 Bb3 and the threat of f5 looms over Black's head. Interesting though is Powell's recommendation of 11...e6 12 Nh4 b5!? 13 Bb3 Nc5 14 f4 0-0-0 when a future a7-a5 must be reckoned with.) 12 Nh4 e6 13 f4 Nb6 14 Bb3 Nbd5 15 Rhf1, and the awkward position of Black's queen bishop is cause for alarm. These variations illustrate some oft-recurring

Diagram 14   After 9 b4

themes in the ...Qa5 variation. Although Black succeeds in deploying his queen bishop actively, its position provokes White into advancing his kingside pawns. Since White can rarely carry out the thematic central breakthrough d5, Black has merely enticed his opponent into the unfoldment of his most logical long-range strategical plan. In this game White's plan is even more effective because White's queen pawn stands on 'd3' rather than 'd4', denying Black any central counterplay. The remainder of the game is an incredible battle 'till the very last move.

9	....	Qb6
10	h4	h6

10...Nxg4? 11 Nd5 Qd6 12 h5 Bf5 13 Nd4 is far too dangerous for Black.

11	h5	Bh7
12	a4	c6
13	g5	hxg5
14	Nxg5	Bg8
15	a5	Qc7
16	b5	cxb5
17	Nxb5	Qc6

Diagram 15   After 17...Qc6

18 Rh3 a6 **19** Nc3 e6 **20** Bb2 Qg2 **21** Qe3 Bc5 **22** d4 Bxd4 **23** Qxd4 Qxg5 **24** Ne4 Nxe4 **25** Qxe4 Bh7 **26** Qd4 Rg8 **27** Re3 Qxh5 **28** Ba3 Qxa5† **29**

29 Kf1 Bf5 30 Rd1 0-0-0 31 Bd6 Qb6 32 Qc3 Qc6 33 Bxa6 Nc5 34 Bxb7†
Kxb7 35 Rb1† Ka8 36 Qxc5 Qh1† 37 Ke2 Bg4† 38 Kd2 Rxd6† 39 Qxd6
Qxb1 40 Ra3† Kb7 41 Rb3† Qxb3 12 cxb3 Bf5 43 Qd7† Kb6 44 Kc3
Rh8 45 Qxf7 Rh3† 46 Kb4 Rh4† 47 Ka3 g6 48 Qf6 Rh3 49 Qd8† Kb5 50
Qb8† Ka5 51 Qa7† Kb5 52 Qb7† Kc5 53 Ka4 Rd3 54 Qc7† Kd5 55 b4 Rd4
56 Ka5 Bd3 57 Qc5† Ke4 58 f3† Black resigns.

Game # 4
Kavalek — Larsen, Beverwijk 1967

1 e4	d5
2 exd5	Qxd5
3 Nc3	Qa5
4 d4	Nf6
5 Bc4	Bg4?!
6 f3!	

6 Nf3 seems weaker: 6...Nc6 7 Bb5 (after 7 h3? Bxf3 8 Qxf3 0-0-0 White
is in trouble; 7 Be3 e5 also gave Black a good game in Bellon — Birescu, Budapest 1978; 7 d5 is complicated but also most likely in Black's favor. A sample
line is 7...0-0-0 8 Bd2 Ne5 9 Be2 Bxf3 10 Bxf3 Nc4 11 0-0 e6 or 9 Bb3
Qa6) 7...0-0-0 (White gained the advantage in Baljon — Bohm, Dutch Championship 1978 after 7...e6? 8 Qd3 Bb4 9 Ne5) 8 Bxc6 bxc6, and on 9 h3
Black has 9...Qh5!

Also possible is 6 Nge2. Black responded aggressively in Whelan — L. Levy,
USA 1976: 6...Nc6 (Black was less enterprising in Donovan — McCormick,
USA 1952, but maintained a solid position following 6...e6 7 0-0 Nbd7 8
Bf4 c6 9 a3 Be7 10 b4 Qd8 11 f3 Bf5 12 Ng3 Bg6) 7 Be3 (7 f3 Bf5 is of
course feasible; 7...Be6 is similar to the line suggested by Miese in Chapter
Three, with the extra move f3 for White) 7...0-0-0 8 f3 e5! with good play.
All this suggests that 6 f3 looks good for White, but the lack of material with
this line makes it difficult to come to a definitive judgement. Unless an improvement is found, however, it looks like Black should enter the main lines
with 5...c6 6 Nf3. For 5...Nc6?!, see B4b2 in Chapter Three.

6	Bf5
7 Nge2	

In Pribyl — Augostin, Poland 1979, the situation became obscure after
7 g4 Bc8 8 Qd3 Nc6 9 Be3 Nb4 10 Qd2 c6. In the present game Black
quickly lands in trouble despite the fact that he has robbed White's king
knight of its best square and provoked the 'weakening' advance f3. Black
never finds the time to exploit White's compromised kingside, and in fact is
pushed back in that sector by White's onrushing foot soldiers.

7	Nbd7

Can 7...Nc6 make this line playable for Black?

8 g4	Bg6

	9 h4	h6
	10 Nf4	e5

After 10...Bh7 a plausible line which looks to be in White's favor is 11 Bd2 c6 12 Ncd5 Qd8 13 Nxf6† Nxf6 14 g5!! hxg5 15 hxg5 Bxc2 16 Rxh8! Bxd1 17 gxf6. But as Larsen himself says, "Long variation, wrong variation!" Is this true here?

11 Nxg6	fxg6
12 Bd2	0-0-0
13 d5	Bb4
14 Qe2	

Diagram 16

After 14 Qe2

14	e4

Black's desire to complicate is understandable in view of alternatives like 14...Nb6 15 0-0-0 Nbxd5 16 Nxd5 Nxd5 17 Bxd5 Rxd5 18 Bxb4 Rxd1† 19 Rxd1 Qxb4 20 Qxe5.

15 fxe4	Ne5
16 0-0-0	Nfxg4

No better for Black is 16...Nxc4 17 Qxc4 Nxg4 18 a3 Bxc3 19 Bxc3 Qb6 20 Bxg7! His opening has failed dismally, but that doesn't stop Larsen from conjuring up ingenious complications. Kavalek, however, exploits his endgame advantage in exemplary fashion.

17 a3	Rhf8
18 Rhf1	Rxf1
19 Rxf1	Bxc3
20 Bxc3	Qc5
21 Bd3	Qe7

21...Rf8 was objectively better, but Black's position would still be wretched. The further opening of the position merely accentuates the bishop's superiority over the knights.

22 Qe1 c6 22 Be2 cxd5 23 exd5 Ne3 25 Rf4! Qc7 26 Re4 N5c4 27 Qg1 Kb8 28 b3 Nxd5 29 Rxc4 Qe7 30 Qh2† Ka8 31 Bb2 Re8 32 Rd4 Ne3 33 Rd2 Nf5 34 Kb1 Nxh4 35 Ka2 g5 36 Bg4 a6 37 Rd7 Qe4 38 Qc7 Nf3

39 Bxf3 Qxf3 40 Rd8† Rxd8 41 Qxd8† Black resigns.

Game #5
Tarrasch — Mieses, Göteborg 1920

1	e4	d5
2	exd5	Qxd5
3	Nc3	Qa5
4	d4	e5
5	Nf3	Bb4
6	Bd2	Bg4
7	Be2	

6 h3 is probably stronger, since Black can now play 7...Nc6. Dr. Tarrasch's play in this game is of such a high standard, however, that it would be criminal to omit this classic from the book.

7	....	exd4
8	Nxd4	Qe5
9	Ncb5!	Bxe2
10	Qxe2	Bxd2†
11	Kxd2	Qxe2†
12	Kxe2	Na6

Can White make something out of his slight lead in development despite the massive simplification?

13	Rhe1	0-0-0

Or 13...Ne7 14 Kf3 Kf8 15 Rad1.

14	Nxa7†	Kb8
15	Nac6†!	

15 Nab5? c6.

Diagram 17

After 15 Nac6†

15	....	bxc6
16	Nxc6†	Kc8
17	Nxd8	Kxd8
18	Rad1†	Ke8
19	Kd3†	Ne7

20	Kc4	h5
21	Rd3	Nb8
22	Rde3	Nbc6
23	b4	f6
24	f4	Kf7
25	a4!	

Not 25 b5? Na5† 26 Kb4 Nd5† 27 Kxa5 Ra8 mate! Now the White queenside pawns roll inexorably forward like army ants, finally devouring Black's cavalry.

25...Rb8 26 c3 Rd8 27 Rd3 Rxd3 28 Kxd3 Ke8 29 a5 Kd7 30 a6 Nd5 31 Ra1 Na7 32 g3 c6 33 Ra4 Nb6 34 Ra5 g6 35 c4 Nbc8 36 Ra1 Nd6 37 Kd4 Ndc8 38 Kc5 Kc7 39 Re1 Nb6 40 Re7† Nd7† 41 Rxd7†! Kxd7 42 b5 cxb5 43 cxb5 Nc8 44 b6 Black resigns.

Game # 6
Karpov — Larsen, Montreal 1979

1	e4	d5
2	exd5	Qxd5
3	Nc3	Qa5
4	d4	Nf6
5	Bd2	

Was Karpov trying to sidestep Larsen's preparation, or was this move decided on before the game? The immediate attempt to harass Black's queen brings White little in this game.

5	....	Bg4

The alternative 5...c6 could easily transpose into a main line after 6 Bc4 Bf5. In Kanshonkov — Kholmov, USSR 1980, the continuation 5...Qb6 6 Nf3 Bg4 7 h3 Bxf3 8 Qxf3 e6 9 0-0-0 c6 10 Bc4 Nbd7 (compare Chapter Five, A.) 11 Rhe1 0-0-0 12 Bf4 Qb4 13 Bb3 Nb6 14 a3 Qe7 15 Bg3 Qd7 resulted in a small plus for White.

6	Be2	Bxe2
7	Ncxe2	Qb6
8	Nf3	Nbd7

The capture of White's 'b' pawn is very dangerous.

9	0-0	e6
10	c4	Be7

The passive positions of White's queen bishop and queen knight severely curtail any ambitions he might have entertained regarding an opening advantage. His seizure of space on the queenside is not much of an accomplishment.

11	b4	0-0
12	a4	c6
13	Qc2	Qc7
14	Rfe1	b6

15	a5	Rfb8
16	a6	b6
17	c5	Nd5
18	Nc1	Re8
19	Nd3	Rad8!
20	g3	Bf6
21	Re4	Nf8
22	h4	Rd7
23	Kg2	Red8

Diagram 18   After 23...Red8

White has gradually consolidated his position and now proceeds to garner territory on the kingside. Black has only one practically invulmerable weakness at c6, however; and when the hand-to-hand fighting begins the voluntary loosening of Karpov's kingside plays a major role in his undoing.

24	g4	Re8
25	g5	Bd8
26	Nfe5	Rde7
27	Bf4	Qc8

Black maneuvers behind the lines with admirable dexterity. All his pieces are poised to rush to a critical sector without delay.

28	Bg3	f6!

Black's only hope for counterplay. This undermining of the e-file is counterbalanced by pressure along the neighboring f-file.

29	Nf3	Rf7
30	Qd2	fxg5!

Black surrenders 'e5', for White can do nothing with it.

31	Nxg5?!	

31 hxg5 was a little better.

31	....	Rf5
32	Ra3	Ng6
33	Nf3	Ref8
34	Nfe5	Nxe5

35 Rxe5	Rf3
36 Ra1?	

White's mobility is curtailed by the need to nursemaid his pawns on a6 and b4. The text move is a serious error which loses material, but alternatives such as 36 Qe2 R3f6 37 Re4 Bc7 38 Bxc7 Qxc7 39 Rxe6 Rxf2†! 40 Nxf2 Nf4† are no better.

36...Bxh4! 37 Qe2 Bxg3 38 fxg3 Qd7 39 Qxf3 Rxf3 40 Kxf3 Nxb4 41 Rd1 Qxd4 42 Re4 Qd5 43 Nf2 Qh5† 44 Kg2 Nd5 45 Rxe6 h6 46 Rd3 Kh7 47 Rf3 b4 48 g4 Qg5 49 Kg3 Qc1 50 Nh3 Qc4 51 g5 h5 52 Re8 h4† 53 Kg2 b3 54 Rb8 Qe2† 55 Nf2 Ne3† White resigns.

Game # 7

Shamkovich — Leverett, USA 1977

1 e4 d5 2 exd5 Qxd5 3 Nc3 Qa5 4 d4 Nf6 5 Nf3 Nc6?! 6 Bb5

6 d5 Nb4 7 Bb5† c6 (7...Bd7 transposes to the game) 8...dxc6 bxc6 9 Ba4 Ba6? (even after the more reasonable 9...Qb6, Qd4! puts White on top) 10 a3! Rd8 11 Bd2 +− was the course of the well-known miniature Fischer — Seidman, USA 1960. Since the present game leaves many questions unanswered, perhaps more attention should be paid to 6 Bd2, e.g., 6...Bg4 7 Nb5 Qb6 8 a4 Bxf3 9 gxf3! (9 Qxf3? a6! 10 a5 axb5! −+) 9...a5 10 Be3 Nd5 11 c4 Nxe3 12 fxe3 Nb4 13 c5 Qc6 14 Nd6†!, etc.

6 .... Bd7

6...Bg4? is easily repulsed by 7 h3. Californean Keith Vickers has demonstrated how Black can leave the books and keep the game complicated if he's willing to take on some dubious positions: Pohl — Vickers, California 1981 went 6...a6 7 Bxc6† bxc6 8 0-0 e6 9 Ne5 Bb7 10 Bg5 Bd6; while Demers — Vickers, California 1981 ran 6...e6!? 7 Ne5 Bb4 8 Bd2 Bxc3 9 Bxc6† bxc6 10 Bxc3 Qd5 11 Qe2 Qxg2 12 0-0-0 Qd5.

7 d5

White could also consider less violent means, e.g., 7 0-0 0-0-0 8 Be3 (8 Bxc6 Bxc6 9 Ne5) 8...Nd5 9 a4 Nxe3 10 fxe3 f6 11 Nd2 e6 12 Na2! which offered him a strong initiative in Mednis — Seidman, USA 1962)

7 .... Nb4

7...Ne5 also deserves a closer look, e.g. 8 Nxe5 (8 Bxd7† Nexd7 with the threat of 9...Nb6) 8...Bxb5 9 Bd2 Ba6.

8 Bd7† Nxd7

9 a3

The threat of ...Nf6 (or Nb6) practically forces White to enter into the coming exchange sacrifice.

9 .... Nf6

(See diagram at top of next page)

10 axb4!?

White gets quite a bit for his material: his pawns cramp Black's position

Diagram 19

and make it difficult for Black to develop his kingside pieces; White leads in development; Black's queen is awkwardly placed. Any yet . . .

10	Qxa1
11 0-0	Rd8

11...Qa6 12 b5 Qd6 13 Qd4 e6 14 Bf4 Qc5 also deserves a test.

12 Nd4	Qa6

Not 12...Nxd5 13 Ndb5 etc.; nor 12...c6 13 dxc6 bxc6 14 Qe2! Rxd4 15 Be3 and White wins; 12...e6 is also inadequate because of 13 Ndb5 Bd6 14 Qe2 Qa6 (14...0-0 15 Be3 Qxb2 16 Rb1) 15 Be3.

13 Ndb5	Rd7
14 Bf4	Kd8?

Far better was 14...Nxd5! 15 Qxd5! Rxd5 16 Nxc7† Kd8 17 Nxa6 Rf5 18 Be3 bxa6 19 Ra1, when White has good play for his material, but the overall situation remains obscure.

15 Qe2!	Nxd5?

The losing move. Black had to try 15...e6 16 Qe5 Qb6! (16...Nxd5 17 Nxd5 Qxb5 18 Bg5†! f6 19 Bxf6† gxf6 20 Qxf6† Ke8 21 Qxe6† Be7 22 Nxe7 etc; or 16...Bd6 17 Nxd6 cxd6 18 Qg5 Rg8 19 Ne4).

16 Nxd5	Rxd5
17 Bxc7†	Kc8

Not much of an improvement is 17...Ke8 18 c4 Rd7 19 Bg3 Qc6 20 Nxa7 Qg6 21 Nb5.

18 c4	Rd7
19 Rd1!	Qe6

Or 19...Rxc7 20 Qd3; 19...Rxd1† 20 Qxd1 b6 21 Qd8† Kb7 22 Qb8† Kc6 23 Nd4†.

20 Rxd7	Qxd7
21 Nxa7†!!	Kxc7
22 Qe5†	Resigns.

Tal — Mascarinas, Lvov 1981

1 e4 d5 2 exd5 Qxd5 3 Nc3 Qa5 4 d4 c6 5 Nf3 Nf6 6 Bd2 Qc7 7 Bc4 e6?!

For 7...Bf5 see games 9 & 10. Best was 7...Bg4.

8 Qe2		Be7
9 g4?!		

Wholly in Tal's style, but White's aggression merely gives Black counterplay later on. The simple 9 0-0 followed by a slow buildup of central pressure would leave Black devoid of active play.

9...Nbd7 10 0-0-0 b5 11 Bd3 b4 12 Ne4 Nd5 13 Kb1 a5 14 g5 Qb6

A good alternative was 14...a4, intending 15...b3.

15 h4		c5

15...Ba6 was also good.

16 dxc5		Nxc5
17 Bb5†		Bd7
18 Bxd7†		Nxd7
19 h5		

Diagram 20

After 19 h5

19		0-0?

A classic example of "castling into it." 19...Qa6! would have maintained equality.

20 g6		h6
21 Bxh6!		f5

21...gxh6 22 Qd2 Kg7 23 gxf7 Kxf7 (23...Rxf7 24 Rhg1† Kh7 25 Rg6 Rf4 26 Rdg1 Bf8 27 Rxe6! etc.; or 25...Bf8 26 Neg5†.) 24 Qxh6 was Black's best, though here, too, White would have an irresistible attack.

22 Rxd5!		exd5

22...fxe4 23 Rxd7 exf3 24 Qe5 wins.

23 Ng3		Rae8

On 23...Bf6 comes 24 Bf4, after which h6 will smash the Black king's defenses.

24 Qd2!		Nc5

25	Bf4	Ne6
26	h6	Rf6
27	hxg7	Nxg7

27...Rxg6 28 Rh8† Kf7 29 Ne5†.

| 28 | Bc7! | |

A typically entertaining Tal game throughout.

| 28 | .... | Qxc7 |
| 29 | Rh8† | Resigns. |

Game # 9

Maroczy — Mieses, Vienna 1908

1 e4 d5 2 exd5 Qxd5 3 Nc3 Qa5 4 d4 Nf6 5 Nf3 Bf5 6 Bc4 c6 7 Bd2 Qc7
8 0-0 e6 9 Ne2 Bd6 10 Ng3 Bg6 11 Re1 Nbd7 12 c3 Rd8 13 Qe2 0-0 14
Rad1

Compare this game with the next, in which White wins by a violent assault.
It seems that even with quiet play in the main ...Qa5 lines White retains a
small but persistent advantage. Black's next move is an error which weakens
'd6', though it takes some fine play by White and a few more slips by Black
before the game ends decisively. Black should have tried 14...c5 or 14...Rfe8.
Great patience is required to handle his position correctly.

14...Bf4?! 15 Ne5 Bxd2 16 Rxd2 Nxe5 17 dxe5 Rxd2 18 Qxd2 Rd8 19
Qe3 Nd7 20 h4 h6 21 h5 Bh7 22 Rd1 Nb6 23 Rxd8† Qxd8 24 Be2 a6 25
c4 Nc8 26 a3 Ne7 27 Qa7! Qc7 28 b4 Nc8 29 Qd4 Kf8 30 Bf3 Ke8 31
Be4 Bxe4 32 Nxe4 Qd7 33 Nd6† Nxd6 34 exd6 f6 35 f4 b5 36 c5 Kd8
37 g4 Qf7 38 Qe4 Kd7 39 Qe2 Qg8 40 Qa2 g6 41 hxg6 Qe8 (41...Qxg6
42 Qxe6†!) **42 f5 Black resigns.**

Game # 10

Korchnoi — Reshko, USSR 1957

1 e4 d5 2 exd5 Qxd5 3 Nc3 Qa5 4 d4 Nf6 5 Nf3 Bf5 6 Bc4 c6 7 Bd2 Qc7

| 8 | Ne5 | e6 |

8...Bg6 may be an improvement.

| 9 | g4! | |

It's unusual to see Korchnoi on the attack so early in the game.

| 9 | .... | Be4 |

If 9...Bg6 10 h4 Bd6, then 11 Qe2.

10 Nxe4 Nxe4 11 Bf4 Nd7 12 Qf3 Qa5† 13 c3 Nef6 14 0-0-0 Nxe5 15
Bxe5 Nd7 16 Bg3 Be7 17 h4

(See diagram at top of next page)

| 17 | .... | Rf8 |

This is a case where Black might have been better off castling into White's
pawn onslaight, in the hope of launching his own attack on the queen's wing.
As it goes, he is soon bereft of counterplay.

18 Rhe1 Nf6 19 Re5 Nd5 20 Bb3 b5 21 Qe2 0-0-0?! 22 Rxe6! fxe6

Diagram 21

After 17 h4

23 Qxe6†   Rd7

23...Kb7 24 Bxd5 cxd5 25 Qxe7† Kc8 26 Qc5† Kb7 27 Re1, etc.
24 Qxc6† Nc7 25 Be6 Rd8 26 d5 Qa6 27 Qxc7 mate.

Game # 11
Spassky — Larsen, Montreal 1979

1 e4 d5 2 exd5 Qxd5 3 Nc3 Qa5 4 d4 Nf6 5 Nf3 Bf5 6 Bd2 Nbd7 7 Bc4 c6 8 Qe2 e6

Black's sixth or seventh moves have been condemned by most annotators, but this may be the real culprit. Worth a try was 8...Qc7 9 Ne5 Bg6, and if 10 Bf4 then 10...Nh5.

9 d5!

White rarely gets a chance to execute this thematic central break. This game shows how devastating his lead in development can be once the position has been opened up.

9 ....   cxd5
10 Nxd5   Qc5

On 10...Qd8 11 Nxf6†, etc.

11 b4 Qc8 12 Nxf6† gxf6 13 Nd4 Bg6 14 h4 h5 15 f4 Be7 16 Rh3! Qc7 17 0-0-0 Qb6 18 Be1 0-0-0

If 18...Bxb4?, then 19 Rb3 wins.

19 Nb5 Nb8 20 Rxd8† Kxd8 21 Bf2 Qc6 22 Bxa7 Nd7 23 a3 Qe4 24 Be3 Bf5 25 Rg3 Qc6 26 Nd4 Qa4 27 Nxf5 Qxa3† 28 Kd1 Qa1† 29 Bc1 Bxb4 30 Bb5 Nb6 31 Qe4 Qa5 32 Qxb7 Black resigns.

Game # 12
J. Marcal — Powell, California 1981

1 e4 d5 2 exd5 Qxd5 3 Nc3 Qa5 4 d4 Nf6 5 Bc4 Bg4 6 Nf3

Stronger is 6 f3 as in game # 4.

6 ....   c6

And here Black might venture 6...Nc6!?

7 Bd2 Nbd7 8 Qe2 Qh5 9 0-0-0 e6

(See diagram at top of next page)

Diagram 22   After 9...e6

Compare this position to those arising after Black's ninth move in the next few games. Black appears to have improved his chances here.

10 Bf4 Nb6 11 Bb3 Be7 12 Be5 0-0 13 h3 Bxf3 14 gxf3 a5 15 a4

15 a3, not surrendering control of b4, would mean that White would have to contend with 15...Nbd5 16 Ne4 b5.

15...Nbd5 16 Ne4 Nxe4 17 Qxe4 Rae8 18 Kb1 Qh6 19 c4 Nb4 20 Rdg1 g6 21 f4 Qh5 22 Ka1 Rc8 23 h4 Rfe8 24 Rg5!? f5

24...Qh6 was better.

25 Rxh5?

Tempting, but White's correct course was 25 Qe3! Bxg5 26 fxg5 Qg4 (else 27 f3) 27 f3 Qg2 28 Rc1! with excellent compensation for the exchange.

25...fxe4 26 Rg1 c5 27 f5 exf5 28 Rxf5 Rf8

White's attack has been broken, but his weak pawns and cornered king remain.

29 Rxf8† Rxf8 30 h5 Rxf2 31 dxc5 Bxc5 32 hxg6 hxg6 33 Rxg6† Kf7 34 Rg1 e3 35 Bd1 e2 White resigns.

Game # 13

Ljubojevic — Kurajica, Bugojno 1980

1 e4 d5 2 exd5 Qxd5 3 Nc3 Qa5 4 Nf3 Nf6 5 d4 Bf5 6 Bd2 c6 7 Bc4 e6 8 Qe2 Bb4 9 0-0-0 Nd5 10 Nxd5 Bxd2† 11 Nxd2 cxd5

Diagram 23   After 11...cxd5

12 Nb3!

Now follows a long, more or less forced series of moves after which White emerges with a much better position. Black's queen remains out of play for a long time, and his king becomes exposed to dangerous threats.

12 ....   Qxa2

Or 12...Qd8 13 Bb5† Nc6 14 Nc5 Qc7 15 Qe5 Qxe5 16 Bxc6† bxc6 17 dxe5 when Black's endgame prospects are dim.

13 Bxd5 Nc6 14 g4 Bg6 15 Bxc6† bxc6 16 f4 0-0 17 h4 h6 18 h5 Bh7 19 g5 Bf5 20 gxh6 gxh6 21 Rhg1† Kh7 22 Rg3 Rg8 23 Rdg1 Rxg3 24 Rxg3 a5

24...Rg8 also fails: 25 Rxg8 Kxg8 26 Qg2† and 27 Qxc6, etc.

25 Qe5 Rg8 26 Rxg8 Kxg8 27 Qxa5 Qxa5 28 Nxa5 Be4 29 Kd2 Kg7 30 c4 Kf6

On 30...Bf3, there follows 31 Ke3 Bxh5 32 Nxc6.

31 Ke3 Bh1 32 b4 Kf5 33 b5 cxb5 34 cxb5 f6 35 Nc4!

As usual, a won game requires care to the end. Not 35 b6? e5 36 b7 exd4† 37 Kxd4 Bxb7 38 Nxb7 Kxf4.

35...Kg4 36 Nd6 Ba8

Also futile was 36...f5 37 b6 Kxh5 38 b7 Bxb7 39 Nxb7 Kg4 40 Nc5 h5 41 Nxe6, etc.

37 b6 Kxh5 38 f5!

38 b7? Bxb7 39 Nxb7 Kg4 = .

38...e5 39 dxe5 fxe5 40 b7 Bxb7 41 Nxb7 Black resigns.

Game # 14

Psahis — Kurajica, Sarajevo 1981

1 e4 d5 2 exd5 Qxd5 3 Nc3 Qa5 4 d4 Nf6 5 Nf3 c6 6 Bc4 Bf5 7 Bd2 e6 8 Qe2 Bb4 9 a3 Bg4

Trying to improve on Velikov — Spiridonov, Bulgarian Championship 1980/81, which went 9...Nd5?! 10 Bxd5! (Fries Nielsen gives "10...Bxc3 = " but 11 Bxc6† 12 Bxc3 wins a pawn) 10...cxd5 11 Qb5† Qxb5 12 Nxb5 Bxd2† 13 Kxd2 Na6 14 Nd6† Ke7 15 Nxf5† with a clear advantage for White.

10 0-0-0 Bxc3 11 Bxc3 Qh5 12 h3?!

Psahis gives "12 d5? Bxf3 13 gxf3 Nxd5 14 Bxg7? Qg5†", but after 14 Bxd5 cxd5 15 Qb5† Black is in a bad way. Probably best is therefore 12 d5! cxd5 13 Bxf6 gxf6 14 Bxf3 Qc5 when White stands slightly better.

12...Bxf3 13 gxf3 Nbd7 14 Rdg1 0-0-0 15 Bd2 Nb6 16 Bb3 Rhg8 17 Rg5 Qh4 18 Ra5 Nfd5!

Not 18...Qxd4?! 19 Be3 and 20 Rxa7.

19 Qe4

The chances hereabouts are even.

(See diagram at top of next page)

Diagram 24   After 19 Qe4

19...Qxf2 20 Rxa7 Nf6 21 Qe3 Qxe3 22 Bxe3 Nfd5 23 Bg5! f6 24 Bd2 g5 25 Re1 Kb8 26 Ra5 Rge8 27 c4 Nf4! 28 Bxf4 gxf4 29 Re4 f5 30 Rxf4 Nd7 31 Rh4 b6 32 Ra4 c5 33 Bc2 cxd4 34 Rxd4 Ne5 35 Rxd8† Rxd8 36 Rb4 Kc7 37 Rb5 Nxf3 38 c5 bxc5 39 Rxc5† Kd6 40 Rc4 Rg8 41 b4 Rg1† 42 Kb2 Rg2 43 b5 Draw.

Game # 15
Jansa — Taulbut, Copenhagen 1981

1 e4 d5 2 exd5 Qxd5 3 Nc3 Qa5 4 d4 Nf6 5 Nf3 c6 6 Bc4 Bf5 7 Bd2 e6 8 Qe2 Bb4 9 Ne5!

This looks like White's strongest move here.

9...Nbd7 10 0-0-0 Nxe5 11 dxe5 Nd7

Also unappetizing for Black is 11...Nd5 12 Bxd5 exd5 13 g4 Bd7 (13...d4 14 Nb1 Bxd2† 15 Rxd2! Be6 16 Rxd4 Qxa2 17 f4 favors White, e.g. 17... Bd5 18 Rhd1 0-0-0 19 c4! etc; 13...Be6!? and now not 14 a3? Bxa3! but 14 f4!? when 14...d4? 15 Ne4 is ±, and 14...Bxc3 15 Bxc3 Qxa2 16 f5 is difficult for Black.) 14 a3 Bxc3 15 Bxc3 Qc7 16 f4.

12 a3 b5 13 Ba2

Or 13 axb4 Qa1† 14 Nb1 bxc4 15 Qxc4 ±.

13 ....   Bxa3

Black does not relish 13...Bxc3 14 Bxc3 Qc7 15 g4 Bg6 16 f4, but his sacrifice must be inadequate.

14 bxc3 Qxa3† 15 Kb1 0-0 16 Bc1 Qb4† 17 Bb2 Nb6 18 Ka1 Rfb8 19 Nb1 Nc4 20 Bc3 Qa4 21 Rd4 Rb6 22 Rxc4 bxc4 23 Qxc4 Qxc2 24 Bd4 Qxc4 25 Bxc4 Rb4 26 Na3 Ra4 27 Ka2?

27 Bc5 maintains White's grip.

27...Rb8 28 Bc3? Be4 29 f3 Rxc4! and Black won in 55 moves.

Game # 16
Duras — Spielmann, Vienna 1907 (Brilliancy Prize)

1 e4 d5 2 exd5 Qxd5 3 Nc3 Qa5 4 d4 Nc6

On 4...c6 5 Nf3 Bg4 6 Be2 Nf6 7 0-0 e6 8 Ne5 (8 h3 Bh5 9 Ne5 Bxe2 10 Qxe2 Be7 11 Bg5 Qd8 12 Rad1 0-0 13 f4 Nd5 = Groszpeter — Rogers,

Skien 1979; but not 10...Nbd7? 11 Re1 Be7? 12 Nxf7! +— Balinas — Donne, Havana 1966) 8...Bxe2 9 Qxe2 Be7 10 Bg5 0-0 11 Rad1 Qc7 12 Rd3 Nbd7 13 Rg3 White obtained kingside pressure in Schlechter — Teichmann, Nuremburg 1896; it increased after 13...g6? 14 h4 Kg7 15 h5.

5 Nf3 Bg4 6 Be2 Nf6 7 Be3 0-0-0 8 Nd2 Bxe2 9 Qxe2 Qf5 10 Nb3

Maroczy — Spielman, 1907 went 10 Nf3 e6 11 0-0-0 Bb4 12 Qc4 Bxc3 13 Qxc3 Nd5 14 Qd3 Qxd3 15 Rxd3 ± .

10 ....   e6?!

Black equalizes after 10...e5! 11 0-0-0 exd4 12 Nxd4 Nxd4 13 Bxd4 Bc5.

11 g3!

This is more exact than 11 0-0-0 Bb4! 12 Qc4 Bxc3 13 Qxc3 Nd5 = .

11...Bd6 12 0-0-0 Nd5 13 Na4

With this move White maintains a slight initiative.

13...e5 14 dxe5 Bxe5

Safer was 14...Nxe3 and 15...Qxe5.

15 Nac5   Nb6?

15...Nxe3 16 fxe3 Rxd1† 17 Rxd1 Rd8 keeps Black in the game.

16 a4   a5

Diagram 25   After 16...a5

17 g4! Qf6 18 c3 Rhe8 19 Nxb7 Rxd1† 20 Rxd1 Bxc3! 21 N7c5! Nb4 22 g5! Qe5 23 Nxa5 h5 24 bxc3 Qxc3† 25 Kb1 Qxc5

Black is counting on 26 Bxc5 Rxe2 but a surprise awaits.

26 Rd8†!   Black resigns.

Game # 17
Korsunski — Arbakov, USSR 1978

1 e4 d5 2 exd5 Qxd5 3 Nc3 Qa5 4 d4 Nf6 5 Nf3 Bg4 6 h3 Bh5 7 Bd2 e6 8 Qe2?!

Unnecessarily allowing messy complications.

8...Nc6! 9 g4 Bg6 10 Bg2 Nb4 11 0-0 Nxc2 12 Rac1 c6 13 a3 Qb6 14 Qc4! Qxb2 15 Ne5 Rc8 16 Qa4 Nxa3 17 Nxc6 bxc6?!

Better was 17...Bc2 18 Qxa7 (18 Rxc2 Qxc2 19 Qxa7 Bd6) 18...bxc6.

18 Bxc6† Kd8 19 Nb1 Bd6 20 Qxa7 Bxb1 21 Ba5† Bc7 22 Qc5 Ne8 23 Bxe8 Kxe8 24 Qc6† Kf8 25 Bxc7 Kg8 26 Qa6 Re8 27 Bd6 Bg6 28 Rc8 f5 29 Bxa3 Qb3 30 Qc6 Kf7 31 Qc7† Kf6 32 Qe5† Kg5 33 Bc1† Kh4 34 Rxe8 Rxe8 25 Qxg7 Black resigns.

Game # 18
Zuckerman — Shamkovich, Cleveland 1975

1 e4 d5 2 exd5 Qxd5 3 Nc3 Qa5 4 d4 Nf6 5 Nf3 Bg4 6 h3 Bh5 7 g4 Bg6 8 Ne5 e6 9 Nc4

In Kokolov — Korolov, USSR 1978, White tried 9 Bd2, which led to an un-clear position after 9...c6 10 Qf3 Bb4 11 Nc4 Qd8 12 0-0-0 Nbd7 13 h4 h5 14 g5 Ng4 15 Qe2 b5.

| 9 .... | Qa6 |
| 10 h4 | |

10 Bf4 Qc6 11 Rg1 Bb4 ∓ .

| 10 .... | Qc6 |
| 11 Rh3 | |

11 f3? Bb4! (11...Nxg4? 12 Ne5 Nxe5 13 Bb5 + −) 12 h5 Be4! ∓
11...Bb4 12 h5 Be4 13 Bd2 Bxc3 14 Rxc3

Diagram 26   After 14 Rxc3

| 14 .... | Qd7? |

This allows White to seize the initiative, whereas 14...Nd5 15 Rb3 h6 was dynamically balanced.

15 f3 Bc6 16 h6! gxh6 17 Bxh6 Nd5 18 Ra3 Qe7 19 g5 Bb5
19...Nd7 20 Na5 ± .
20 Qd2 Nc6 21 Nb6 Nxb6 22 Bxb5 Qd6 23 0-0-0 Rg8 24 Qe2 a6 25 Bxc6† Qxc6 26 Rc3 Qd6 27 Qe4 Nd5 28 Rb3 0-0-0 29 c4 Qc6 30 Qxh7 Qxc4† 31 Kb1 f5 32 gxf6 Nxf6 33 Qf7 Qe2?? 34 Rc1 Nd5 35 Bf4 Black resigns.

Game # 19
Karpov — Larsen, Buenos Aires 1982

1 e4 d5 2 exd5 Qxd5 3 Nc3 Qa5 4 Nf3 Nf6 5 d4 Bg4 6 h3 Bh5 7 g4 Bg6 8 Ne5 e6 9 Bg2 c6 10 h4 Nbd7 11 Nc4

11 Nxd7 Kxd7 12 h5 Be4 13 Bxe4 Nxe4 14 Qf3 Nxc3 (14...Nd6 15 Bf4)
15 bxc3 Be7 leads to an unclear position, as does 11 h5 Nxe5 (11...Be4!? 12
Nc4 Qa6) 12 dxe5 Qxe5† (not 12...Bxc2? 13 Qxc2 Qxe5† 14 Ne2! Nxg4
15 Bf4 ±) 13 Qe2 (13 Kf1 Rd8!, but not 13...Be4? 14 Nxe4 Nxe4 15 Qe1!
f5 16 f3 and White wins.) 13...Qxe2† 14 Kxe2 Bxc2 15 Kd2 Nxg4. Extremely interesting is 11 Nxd7 Kxd7 12 Bd2 h6 13 d5! exd5 14 Nxd5 Re8†
15 Ne3 Qa4! (and not 15...Qa6? 16 Bf1 b5 17 a4).

11	....	Qa6
12	Bf1	b5
13	h5	

Diagram 27   After 13 h5

13...Bxc2 14 Qxc2 bxc4 15 g5 Nd5 16 Qe4 Rb8
A very explosive, obscure tactical situation has arisen.
17 Rh3 Be7 18 Be2 Rb6 19 Kf1 Nf8 20 Nd1 Qa4 21 Bd2 Bb4 22 Bf4 Nd7
23 Bh2 Be7 24 Rc1 Qxa2 25 Be5?! c3! 26 bxc3 Nxe5 27 Qxe5 0-0??
27...Ba3!?; 27...Rg8!?.
28 h6 f6 29 Qxe6† Kh8 30 hxg7† Kxg7 31 Bd3 Rh8 32 c4 Black resigns.

Game # 20
P. Whitehead — C. Powell, San Francisco 1982
1 e4 d5 2 exd5 Qxd5 3 Nc3 Qa5 4 d4 Nf6 5 Nf3 Bg4 6 h3 Bh5 7 g4 Bg6
8 Ne5 e6 9 Bg2 c6 10 0-0 Nbd7
The alternatives are 10...Be7 and 10...Bb4. In view of the danger to Black's
queen bishop from the advance of White's king bishop pawn, the latter is
probably Black's best, as it fights for control of e4. On the other hand, White
might play 11 f4!? anyway, since 11...Bxc3 12 bxc3 Qxc3 13 Nxg6! hxg6
(13...Qxa1 14 Nxh8 & Nxf7) 14 Rb1 gives him fantastic play for the pawn.
11 Nxg6
This throws away some of White's advantage. 11 f4! is correct, when
11...0-0-0 12 Qf3! threatens various sacrificial explosions on c6. Perhaps
Black should play 11...Bb4 but not exchange on c3 until he is provoked into
doing so.

11...hxg6 12 Bf4 Bb4 13 Ne2 0-0 14 a3 Be7 15 c4 Qa6 16 Qc2 Rac8 17 b4 b5 18 c5 Qb7 19 Bd2 Nd5 20 f4 ± / ±

Diagram 28   After 20 f4

20...Bf6 21 Qd3 Rfe8 22 Ng3 Be7 23 Rae1 Rcd8 24 f5 Nf8 25 fxe6 Nxe6 26 Rxe6 fxe6 27 Qxg6 Rf8 28 Qxe6† Kh8 29 Nf5 Bf6 30 Qe4 g6 31 Ng3 Qg7 32 Ne2 Qe7 33 Qxe7 Nxe7 34 Be3 Kg8 35 Rd1 Rfe8 36 Bf2 Nd5 37 Bxd5† Rxd5 38 Nf4 Rd7 39 Kg2 Kf7 40 Kf3 Red8 41 Ne2 g5 42 a4 a6 43 axb5 axb5 44 Ra1 Rh8 45 Ra6 Rxh3† 46 Kg2 Rb3 47 Rxc6 Rxb4 48 Rb6 Re7 49 Nc3 Bxd4 50 Nxb5 Bxf2 51 Nd6† Ke6 52 Rxb4 Bxc5 White resigns.

Game # 21

Fischer — Addison, Palma de Mallorca 1970

1 e4 d5 2 exd5 Qxd5 3 Nc3 Qd8 4 d4 Nf6 5 Bc4
    Szabo — Fuster, 1951 was very similar to the Fischer game. After 5 Bg5 Bf5 6 Qf3 Qc8 7 Bc4 c6 8 Nge2 Bxc2 9 0-0 Bg6 10 Ng3 Nbd7 11 Rfe1 White had a powerful initiative.

          5 ....   Bf5?!
    Parma — Germek, Bled 1961, went 5...c6 6 Nf3 Bf5 7 Ne5 e6 (7...Bg6!?) 8 0-0 (8 g4!?) 8...Nbd7 9 Qe2 Be7 10 Rd1 Nd5 11 Ne4 0-0 12 Ng3 Nxe5?! (correct was 12...Bg6 ±) 13.dxe5 Bg6 14 Bd3 Qc7 15 Bxg6 hxg6 16 c4 ± ; 5...Bg4 6 f3 Bc8 (6...Bf5 is untried. Compare game # 4) 7 Bg5 e6 8 f4! Nbd7 9 Nf3 Nb6 10 Bb3 a5 11 a4 Be7 12 0-0 0-0 13 Qe2 c6 14 Rad1 was ± in Fuderer — Bronstein, 1959.
6 Qf3! Qc8 7 Bg5 Bxc2 8 Rc1 Bg6 9 Nge2 Nbd7 10 0-0 e6 11 Bxf6 gxf6
    The reply to Nxf6 is the same.
12 d5 e5 13 Bb5 Be7 14 Ng3 a6 15 Bd3 Qd8 16 h4! h5 17 Bf5 Nb6 18 Nce4 Nxd5 19 Rfd1 c6 20 Nc3 Qb6 21 Rxd5! cxd5 22 Nxd5 Qxb2 23 Rb1 Qxa2 24 Rxb7 Black resigns.

Game # 22

Fischer — Robatsch, Varna Olympiad 1962

1 e4 d5 2 exd5 Qxd5 3 Nc3 Qd8 4 d4 g6 5 Bf4!

This game, and this move, have put 4...g6 on the sidelines for two decades.

	5	Bg7

5...Nh6 6 Be5!

	6 Qd2!	

Now 6...Qxd4 7 Qxd4 Bxd4 8 Nb5 Bb6 9 Nxc7† Bxc7 10 Bxc7 or 6...Bxd4 7 0-0-0 Nc6 8 Bb5 Bd7 9 Nd5! (not 9 Bxc6? Bxc6 10 Qxd4? Qxd4 11 Rxd4 Bxg2) 9...e5 10 Nf3 both leave Black in a bad way, so instead Black tries quieter means, though he gets smashed just the same.

6...Nf6 7 0-0-0 c6 8 Bh6 0-0?

White's attack is now irresistable.

9 h4 Qa5 10 h5! gxh5 11 Bd3 Nbd7 12 Nge2 Rd8 13 g4 Nf8 14 gxh5 Ne6 15 Rdg1 Kh8 16 Bxg7† Nxg7 17 Qh6 Rg8 18 Rg5 Qd8 19 Rhg1 Nf5 20 Bxf5 Black resigns.

Game # 23
Karpov — Lutikov, USSR 1979

1 e4 d5 2 exd5 Qxd5 3 Nc3 Qd6 4 d4 Nf6 5 Nf3 a6 6 Be3 Nc6 7 Qd2 Bg4

7...Bf5!?.

	8 Ng5!	

8 Be2!?

	8	e5
	9 d5	Nb4

Diagram 29   After 9...Nb4

10 f3 Bf5 11 Nge4 Qd7 12 0-0-0 c6

12...0-0-0 13 Bc4 still leaves Black facing the threat of a3.

13 dxc6 Qxd2† 14 Rxd2 Bxe4?

Now the two bishops, White's queenside majority, and Black's weak pawns and White squares add up to a decisive White advantage. Better was 14...Nxc6 15 Bc4 ±.

15 Nxe4 Nxc6 16 Nxf6† gxf6 17 Bd3 0-0-0 18 Rhd1 Kc7 19 c3 h5 20 Bf5 Rxd2 21 Rxd2 Nb8 22 h4 Bh6 23 Bxh6 Rxh6 24 a4 Rh8 25 b4 b6 26 b5 Rg8 27 Kc2 axb5 28 axb5 Re8 29 c4 Black resigns.

Part Two

Chapter One

1 e4	d5
2 exd5	Nf6

Diagram 30   After 2...Nf6

As in the Alekhine Defense, Black will allow White to develop a full pawn center in the hopes of achieving counterplay by attacking it.

3 c4

3 b3!?, though interesting, should not give White any advantage, e.g. 3... Nxd5 4 Bb2 Nc6 (4...c5!?) 5 g3 (5 d4!? Bf5 6 a3! e6 7 c4 Nf6 8 Nf3 Bg4 9 Nbd2 Qd7 10 Be2) 5...e5 6 Bg2 g6 7 Ne2 Bg7 with easy play for Black.

3 .... c6!

Best. Other moves give Black inadequate play for the pawn: i. 3...e6? 4 dxe6 Bxe6 5 d4 is a disaster for Black; ii. 3...c5?! 4 Nf3 (4 d4 looks good but is met by the surprising 4...e6! 5 dxe6 cxd4 6 exf7† Kxf7 with attacking chances based on the cramping pawn on d4 and his lead in development.) 4...e6 5 dxe6 Bxe6 6 d3 (6 d4 cxd4 7 Qxd4 Nc6 8 Qxd8† Rxd8 gives Black compensation for his pawn.) 6...Nc6 7 Be2 Qd7 8 0-0 0-0-0 9 a3 (Also good is 9 Nc3 Bf5 10 Qa4 Bd6 11 Bg5 h6 12 Bxf6 gxf6 13 Nd5 Bb8 14 Rfe1 Qd6 15 g3 Chasin — Miazakanjan, 1965) 9...Bd6 10 Nc3 h6 11 b4! Bb8 12 bxc5 Bg4 Szily — Tapaszto, Budapest 1954, and now 13 Nb5! would give White a clear advantage.

4 dxc6

(See diagram at top of next page)

A risky variation for White, who, for a pawn, gives Black a lead in development, control of the d4 square, and great attacking chances. Much safer is 4 d4 cxd5 transposing into a Caro-Kann, Panov-Botvinnik Attack.

The unusual 4 Qa4 would also transpose into a Caro-Kann after 4...Bd7 5 Qb3 cxd5 6 cxd5 Na6! (The Caro move order is: 1 e4 c6 2 c4 d5 3 cxd5 cxd5 4 exd5 Nf6 5 Qa4† Bd7 6 Qb3 Na6.

Diagram 31   After 4 dxc6

4	Nxc6

A. 5 Nf3?!; B. 5 d3.

A.

5 Nf3?!	e5
6 d3	

6 Nc3? e4 7 Ng5 Bf5 8 Be2 (For 8 f3 see game # 1) 8...h6 9 Nh3 g5 10 g4? Bg6 11 Qa4 Bd6 12 Nd5 0-0 13 f4 exf3 14 Bxf3 Nxd5 15 cxd5 Re8† 16 Kf2 Nb4 0 - 1, Kosulejeva — Gaprindashvili, USSR 1960.

6	e4

6...Bf5 is game # 2, while 6...Bc5 is game # 3.

7 dxe4	

7 Ng5 Bb4† 8 Nc3 Bg4 9 Qc2 (9 Qd2 Qa5 10 Ngxe4? Nxe4 11 dxe4 Rd8 is horrid, while 9 Be2 Bxe2 10 Qxe2 Qxd3 or 9 f3 exf3 10 Nxf3 0-0 11 Be2 Qb6 are both favorable to Black.) 9...Nd4 10 Qd2 (10 Qa4† Bd7 11 Qd1 is stronger) 10...Qa5 11 Ngxe4 0-0-0 was crushing in the game Maksudov — Mergelishvili, USSR 1961.

7	Qxd1†
8 Kxd1	Nxe4
9 Be3	Bg4
10 Be2	0-0-0†
11 Kc1	

11 Nbd2? loses a piece to 11...Bxf3 12 Bxf3 Nxd2 13 Bxd2 Bb4; while 11 Nfd2 led to a quick loss after 11...Bf5 12 a3 Bc5 13 Bxc5 Nxc5 14 Kc1 Nd4 0 - 1, Aut — Nikonowa, USSR 1965.

11	Bc5
12 Bxc5	Nxc5
13 Nc3	Nb4
14 Rd1	Bf5

Threatens a pretty mate by 15...Nxa2† and 16...Nb3.

15 Nd5?	Ncd3†
16 Bxd3	Nxd3†
17 Kd2	Nxb2

51

18 Rdc1	Kb8
19 Kc3	Nxc4
20 Kxc4	Be6
21 Rd1	Rd7
22 Ng5	Rc8† — +

It is clear that White's play has met with disaster. It is not hard to con-
clude that 5 Nf3 is a weak move which allows Black fine chances based on a
e5-e4 push.

B.
5 d3

The most flexible move. 5 Nc3 e5 6 d3 amounts to the same thing.

| 5 .... | e5 |
| 6 Nc3 | |

B1. 6...Bf5; B2. 6...Bc5.

B1.
| 6 .... | Bf5 |
| 7 Nf3 | |

B1a. 7...Qd7; B1b. 7...e4?; B1c. 7...Bc5; B1d. 7...Bb4.

B1a.
| 7 .... | Qd7 |

A logical move. Black prepares to castle queenside and immediately win
back his pawn. Analysts though have argued that White can ignore the loss of
his extra pawn and instead play for control of the d5 square by eradicating
Black's f6 knight by Bg5 and Bxf6. Improvements, though, may well be possible, and the final verdict of 7...Qd7 is not at all clear.

| 8 Be2 | 0-0-0 |

8...Rd8 9 0-0 Bxd3 10 Bxd3 Qxd3 11 Qa4 ±, analysis by Lasker.

9 0-0	Bxd3
10 Bxd3	Qxd3
11 Qa4	Bc5

11...h6 12 Be3 favors White.

| 12 Bg5 | h6?! |

This move and the main line are an analysis by Lasker done in 1909, but
can 12...h6 be right? More logical seems to be 12...Qg6!? (12...Qf5!?), then
13 Qb5!? (13 Bxf6 gxf6 14 Qb5 Bd6 followed by 15...Rhg8 & 16...f5 should
give Black ample play) 13...e4!? (13...Bd6) 14 Ne5 (14 Qxc5 exf3 15 g3)
14...Qxg5 15 Nxc6 a6! (not 15...Bxf2†?? 16 Rxf2 Qxb5 17 Nxa7† +—;
but 15...bxc6 16 Qxc6† Kb8 17 Qb5† Ka8 18 b4 Bxf2† 19 Rxf2 Qxb5, is
interesting.) 16 Qa4 bxc6 17 Qxc6† Kb8 seems good for Black since White
can no longer check on b5, e.g. 18 Nd5 Rc8 19 Qxa6 Nxd5 or 18 Qxa6 Rd6.

| 13 Bxf6 | gxf6 |
| 14 Nd5 | |

White's position is preferable (Lasker). Play might continue 14...Rhg8

15 Qb3! Qf5 16 Nh4 Qe6 17 Qf3 ± .

B1b.

7	....	e4?
8	Nh4	Bg4
9	Be2	Bxe2
10	Qxe2	Qxd3
11	Qxd3	exd3
12	0-0	0-0-0
13	Bg5	

White is better. (Analysis by Lasker.)

B1c.

7	....	Bc5
8	Be3	

8 Bg5 is interesting. After 8...Qb6 9 Qd2 Ng4 10 Bh4 White has nothing to fear. Schwarz has recommended 9...0-0-0! White should then avoid the blunder 10 Bxf6 gxf6 11 Nd5? Rxd5! 12 cxd5 Bb4 and may instead try 10 Na4 Qb4 11 Nxc5 Qxc5 but it seems that here too Black has good compensation for his pawn, e.g. 12 Be3 (12 Bxf6 gxf6 13 0-0-0 Nb4) 12...Qe7 leaves Black with threats such as ...e5-e4; ...Bxd3; ...Nb4.

8	....	Qb6!

8...Bxe3 9 fxe3 Qb6 10 Qd2 0-0-0 (10...e4!? 11 Nh4 Be6 threatening 12...g5.) 11 Nh4? Bxd3 12 Bxd3 e4 13 Nxe4? Nxe4 14 Qe2 Qb4† 15 Kf1 Rxd3 16 Qg4† (16 Qxd3 Qxb2) 16...f5 17 Qxf5† Kb8 18 Qxe4 Qxb2 Ermilov — Steinbook, 1961. White's game was falling apart. But 11 0-0-0! is not at all clear: 11...e4 (11...Bxd3 12 Bxd3 e4 12 Qe2 favors White) 12 Nh4 (12 Ng5 Ne5 13 d4 h6 14 Qf2 may be even stronger.) 12...Bg4 13 Be2 is complicated but should be good for White.

9	Qd2	Rd8!

A game Agrinski — Iljagujev, 1961 saw White get some advantage after 9...0-0 10 Na4 Bxe3 11 fxe3 Qb4 12 Qxb4 Nxb4 13 e4 Bd7 14 Nc3 Nc2† 15 Kd2 Nxa1 16 Nxe5 b5 17 Be2 bxc4 18 Nxc4 Be6 19 Rxa1 Rfd8 20 b3.

After 9...Rd8! Black has excellent chances.

B1d.

7	....	Bb4

Considered best by Boleslavski.

8	Be2	e4
9	Nh4	

9 dxe4 Qxd1† 10 Kxd1 Nxe4 should be avoided by White.

9	....	Be6
10	0-0	

10 Bg5 h6.

10	....	exd3

53

11	Bxd3	Bxc3
12	bxc3	Ne5
13	Be2	Qxd1
14	Rxd1	Rc8

Black stands well.

B2.

6	....	Bc5
7	Be3	

A possible alternative is 7 Bg5!? 0-0 8 Nf3 which is untested. White should be careful to avoid ultra aggression by 8 Nd5?? (8 Ne4?? Nxe4!) as 8...Nxd5! splatters him: 9 cxd5 (9 Bxd8 Bb4† 10 Qd2 Bxd2† 11 Kxd2 Rxd8 leaves White dreaming of a draw.) 9...Qxg5 10 dxc6 Bb4† 11 Ke2 e4 12 d4 (12 dxe4 Rd8 followed by Rd2†) 12...bxc6 13 Qc1 Ba6† 14 Kd1 Qxc1† 15 Rxc1 Bxf1 0 - 1.

7	....	Bxe3

7...Nd4 was tried in Trifunovic — Maric, Yugoslavia 1953; after 8 Nf3 0-0 9 Be2 Bf5 10 Bxd4 exd4 11 Nb1 b5 12 Nbd2 bxc4 13 Nxc4 Nd5 14 0-0 Re8 15 a3 Nf4 16 Re1 Qf6 17 Bf1 Bg4 an obscure position resulted.

8	fxe3	Qb6
9	Qd2	Be6
10	e4	

Diagram 32   After 10 e4

Some sources give this position as being favorable to White, but after :

10	....	Ng4!

Black seems to gain full compensation for his pawn.

Other moves leave White with the advantage: i. 10...0-0 11 Nf3 Rad8 12 Nd5 Bxd5 13 cxd5 Nb4 14 a3 (14 Nxe5? Rfe8 15 Nc4 Qc5 16 Be2 Nxe4! 17 dxe4 Rxe4 leaves Black with a strong attack.) 14...Na6 15 b4! Mannke — Doda, correspondence 1960. ii. 10...Rd8 11 Nd5 Bxd5 12 cxd5 Nxd5 13 exd5 Rxd5 14 Qc3? 0-0 15 Ne2 Nb4 16 Rd1 Rfd8 17 Nc1 Rc5! Lave — Duhrssen, correspondence 1928 was winning for Black (18 Qb3 Nc2†

19 Kd2 Qh6†). Instead of the pathetic 14 Qc3 White should play 14 0-0-0! when Black would have a real problem in proving his sacrifice sound.

	11 Nd5

11 Nd1 Nxh2!

	11	**Bxd5**
	12 exd5	**Nd4**

With ...Ne3 to come, Black can look to the future with confidence (13 0-0-0? Nf2! 14 Qxf2? Nb3†).

Chapter Two

	1 e4	**d5**
	2 exd5	**Nf6**
	3 Bb5†	

Diagram 33   After 3 Bb5†

This sharp move leads to tactical situations in which White often makes an effort to hold on to his extra pawn. Though better motivated than Chapter One, Black's resources here too must be considered entirely adequate.

A. 3...c6?!; B. 3...Nbd7; C. 3...Bd7.

A.

	3	**c6?!**

This overly forcing move does not give Black adequate compensation for the pawn.

	4 dxc6	**bxc6**
	5 Bc4	

For the solid alternative 5 Be2 see game # 4.

	5	**e5**
	6 d3	**Bc5**
	7 Nf3	

7 Be3? gives Black good compensation after 7...Bxe3 8 fxe3 Qb6 9 Qc1 Ng4 10 Ke2 0-0 (To be avoided is 10...Nxe3? 11 Qxe3 Qxb2 12 Nf3 Qxa1 13 Nxe5 0-0 14 Rf1 Be6 15 Nd2 Qc3 16 Bxe6 fxe6 17 Rxf8† Kxf8 18 Qf4† Mieses — Tartakower, 1907).

A good alternative for White is 7 Nc3 0-0 8 Nf3 Bg4 9 0-0 Nbd7 10 Qe2 Qc7 11 h3 Bh5 12 Be3 Bb4 13 g4 Nxg4 14 hxg4 Bxg4 15 Ne4 Kh8 16 Kg2! f5 17 Rh1! fxe4 (17...h6 18 Bxh6) 18 Rxh7† Kxh7 19 Rh1† Kg6 20 Nh4† with a quick win in sight, Krüger — Sahlmann, 1938.

7	....	Ng4	
8	0-0	0-0	

8...e4? 9 Qe2.

9 Nc3

Black has insufficient compensation for the pawn.

B.

3	....	Nbd7!?

There is not much experience with this move, the few cases of its use tending to favor Black. If it needs a label, then 'unclear' is perhaps best.

4 c4

Holding on to the pawn. In the game Vauner — Resko, USSR, Black did very well after 4 Nc3 a6 5 Bxd7† Qxd7! 6 Qf3 b5 7 d6 Ra7 8 dxe7 Bxe7 9 Nge2 Bb7 10 Qe3 c5 11 0-0 b4 12 Nd1 0-0 13 d3 Re8 14 Nf4 Bd6 15 Qh3 Qc7 16 Nh5 Nxh5 17 Qxh5 Re6! with fine attacking chances.

4	....	a6

5 Bxd7†

5 Ba4 b5 6 cxb5 Nxd5 7 Nc3 Bb7 8 Nxd5 Bxd5 9 Nf3 axb5 10 Bxb5 c6 11 Be2 Nc5 threatening 12...Nb3 left Black with more than enough for the pawn in Anguiano — Wieter, Mexico 1978.

5	....	Qxd7

6 d3

6 Nc3? c6 7 dxc6 Qxc6 allows Black to regain his pawn.

6	....	c6

An important alternative is 6...b5!?. Schumacher — Eudokimov, corr. 1955 saw Black gain an advantage after 7 Qe2 bxc4 8 dxc4 c6 9 dxc6 Qxc6 10 Nf3 Bb7 11 Na3 0-0-0 12 Nc2 e5 13 0-0 Bd6 14 Rd1? Ng4!. Larsen offers 14 Bg5 as an improvement with the assessment of 'unclear'. Schwarz feels that 7 Qe2 is the culprit and recommends 7 Nf3 as leading to a White advantage. I feel this is far from clear though, after 7...bxc4 8 dxc4 c6 9 dxc6 Qxc6 Black's pieces will become very active. An honest assessment awaits future tests.

7	dxc6	Qxc6

8 Nf3

The game Fuderer — Bogoljubov, Belgrade 1952 saw White try 8 Qf3?! but after 8...Qc7 9 Nge2 Bg4 10 Qg3 e5 an obscure position arose in which Black's chances must be deemed equal to White's.

8	....	Bg4

9 0-0

Another untested position. Black has compensation, but is it enough? Perhaps ±.

C.

            3 ....   Bd7

Diagram 34   After 3...Bd7

This is the most popular reply, insuring Black good chances.

C1. 4 Bxd7†?!; C2. 4 Be2; C3. 4 Bc4.

C1.
4 Bxd7†?!

This illogical move has a bad reputation, and rightly so! Much of the tension is taken out of the position by a capture that only aids Black's development. The point of 3 Bb5† is to tangle Black's pieces up by forcing him to put his bishop on the unfavorable d7 square.   That White now solves Black's problem by exchanging . . .

            4 ....   Qxd7
            5 c4

5 Nf3 Nxd5 6 d4 Qe6†! is very comfortable for Black.

5...c6 6 dxc6 Nxc6 7 Nf3 e5 8 0-0 Bc5

For the highly interesting 8...e4! see game # 5.

9 d3 0-0-0 10 Nc3 Qxd3 11 Qxd3 Rxd3 12 Bg5! e4 = .

C2.
4 Be2

A quiet continuation which draws the game back into positional lines. Often called harmless, Black's road to equality is not as simple as many books would have you think.

            4 ....   Nxd5
            5 d4

C2a. 5...g6; C2b. 5...Bf5.

C2a.
            5 ....   g6

Black has certain difficulties after this move. Alternatives are: i. 5...e6

6 c4! (to prevent c7-c5) 6...Nf6 (6...Bb4†? 7 Kf1! Nf6 8 c5! c6 9 Qb3 wins material) 7 Bg5 Be7 8 Nf3 White has the more comfortable position;

ii. 5...Nc6!? 6 c4 Nf6 7 Nc3 e5 8 dxe5 Nxe5 9 Nf3 Nxf3† 10 Bxf3 c6 11 0-0 Be6! = Stephenson — Karaklaic, 1962. Instead 7 d5 Ne5 8 Nf3 favors White. In turn, Black could try 6...Nb6 when 7 Nf3 Bg4 transposes to positions considered in Chapter Three, B3b2. After 6...Nb6, 7 d5 is sharper, when 7...Ne5 8 c5 Nc8 leaves the position unclear . . . is White overextended or is Black running out of space?

6 c4

i. 6 Nf3 led to quiet play and a slight edge to White after 6...Bg7 7 0-0 0-0 8 c3 Nc6 9 Na3! Matulovic — Zichichi, Venice 1969.

ii. 6 Nc3 Nxc3 7 bxc3 Bg7 8 Nf3 0-0 9 Bf4 c5 10 Be5 f6 11 Bg3 Qa5 12 Qd2 Nc6 13 Bc4† Kh8 14 d5 f5 15 0-0 Bxc3 16 Qe2 Nd4 17 Nxd4 Bxd4 18 Rab1 ± Lukin — Manin, USSR 1963. Black can play more accurately by 8...c5! 9 Bf4 Qa5 10 Qd2 Nc6.

6	Nb6

Possible is 6...Nf6. A game Ravinsky — Jalimbeili, USSR 1964 continued 7 Nc3 Bg7 8 Nf3 0-0 9 0-0 c5 10 d5 Na6 11 Bg5 Ne8 12 Qd2 f6 13 Bf4 Nd6 14 Rfe1 Bg4 15 b3 Nc7 16 Rac1 Nf7 17 Ng5! Bxe2 18 Bxc7 Qxc7 19 Ne6 +— . Black's play was very poor here, but in general the knight placed on f6 offers little counterplay to the second player in such positions.

7 Nc3	Bg7

Schwarz gives 7...c6 8 c5 Nd5 9 Qb3!

8 c5	Nc8
9 d5	

Suetin tried 9 Bf4 against Lutikov in 1960 but could make no headway after 9...0-0 10 Bf3 (10 Nf3!?) 10...Nc6 11 Nge2 e5 12 dxe5 Nxe5 13 Be4 c6 14 0-0 Be6 15 Qxd8 Rxd8 16 Rfd1 Ne7 17 Rac1 f5 18 Bc2 Kf7 19 b3 Nd5 20 Nxd5 Rxd5 21 Rxd5 Bxd5 22 f3 Re8 23 Kf2 Nd7 ½ - ½ .

9	c6
10 Qb3	

Diagram 35

After 10 Qb3

An unusual position!

10	b6
11 Bf3	0-0

11...bxc5? 12 Qb7 Nb6 13 dxc6 Bc8 14 c7! + − .

12 Be3 cxd5 13 Bxd5 Nc6 14 Rd1 Qc7 15 Nb5 Qb7 16 Nd4 Rb8?

Black had to try 16...e5!

17 Ngf3	e5

17...e6 18 Nxe6 fxe6 19 Bxe6† wins.

18 Bxf7†!	Rxf7
19 Nxc6	Bxc6

19...Qxc6 20 Ng5 Be8 21 Nxf7 Bxf7 22 Rd8† Bf8 23 Bh6!

20 Rd8†	Bf8
21 Nxe5	bxc5

21...Kg7 22 Nxf7 Qxf7 23 Bh6‡!

22 Bh6!	+ −

Bronstein − Lutikov, USSR 1960.

C2b.

5	Bf5

This should equalize.

6 Nf3	e6

This position can also be reached in Chapter Three after 1 e4 d5 2 exd5 Nf6 3 d4 Nxd5 4 Nf3 Bf5 5 Be2 e6 . . . same position, different move number!

7 0-0	

For 7 a3!? see game # 6 for a fine example of the effective use of White's space advantage.

7	Be7

7...Bd6 allows White the option of gaining time by a later c4-c5 advance: 8 c4 Nf4? (8...Nf6 keeps White's advantage down to a minimum) 9 c5 Nxe2† 10 Qxe2 Be7 11 Qb5†, etc.

8 c4	

8 a3 0-0 (8...Nc6 9 c4 Nb6 10 Nc3 Bg4 11 d5! ± Savon − Dzindzihasvili, USSR 1971) 9 c4 Nb6 (9...Nf6! 10 Nc3 Ne4 is supposed to lead to easy equality . . . why then is it avoided with such regularity?) 10 Nc3 Nc6 11 h3 (Bronstein tried to avoid h3 in order to have time to support his center but he also gained no advantage: 11 Be3 Bg4 12 b3 Bf6 13 Ne4 Bxf3 14 Nxf6† Qxf6 15 Bxf3 Rfd8 16 Bxc6 bxc6 17 Qg4 ½ - ½, Bronstein − Gipslis, Tallinn '75) 11...Bf6 12 Be3 Qd7 13 b4 Rfd8 14 Ra2 Nxd4 15 Nxd4 Bxd4 16 Rd2 e5 17 Nb5 Be6 18 Nxd4 exd4 19 Rxd4 Qe8 20 Qc2 Rxd4 21 Bxd4 White's two bishops give him a minimal edge, but Black's pressure on the White 'c' pawn allows him to hold the balance: 21...f6 22 Re1 Bf7 23 Qb1 Bg6 24 Qa1 Qf7 25 Bf3 c6 26 b5 Re8 27 Bxb6 axb6 = Lutikov − Gipslis, Dubna 1976

8 ....   **Nb4!**

8...Nf6!?; 8...Nb6 9 Nc3 Nc6 left White with a clear advantage after 10 d5 exd5 11 cxd5 Nb4 12 Nd4 Bc8 (12...Bg6? 13 f4!) 13 Bf3 0-0 (13...N6xd5 14 Nxd5 Nxd5 15 Re1 with attacking prospects) 14 Nc2 Bf5 15 Nxb4 Bxb4 16 Qd4 Qe7 17 Bd2 Bc5 18 Qf4 Matanovic — Karaklaic, Belgrade 1954. White soon won material after 18...Qf6 19 Nb5 Bd3 20 Qxf6 gxf6 21 Rfc1 Bd6 22 Nxd6 cxd6 23 Rc7 Bc4 24 Rxb7 Bxd5 25 Rxb6 Bxf3 26 Rxd6 Be4 27 Rxf6. Perhaps 9...0-0 is better, with 10...Nc6 to follow. (Though here too White could try 10 d5.)

9 Na3   0-0

Also playable is 9...N8c6 10 Be3 0-0 11 Qb3 a5 12 Rfd1 Honfi — Dely, Hungary 1973, and now 11...a4! should be satisfactory for Black.
10 Qb3 a5 11 Rd1 c6 12 Bf4 Nd7 13 Ne1 Nf6 = Kupreichik — Didishko, USSR 1969.

C3.
4 Bc4

Diagram 36   After 4 Bc4

The point of 3 Bb5†. Black will experience difficulty in regaining his pawn. In compensation, Black will have a lead in development and will often end up with a more compact pawn structure (C3c.).

C3a. 4...c6; C3b. 4...b5!?; C3c. 4...Bg4!.

C3a.
4 ....   c6

As usual, this is unsound.

5 dxc6   Nxc6
6 Nf3

An analysis by Kolozeiczika shows that 6 d4 e5! 7 dxe5 Nxe5 8 Qe2 Bb4† 9 c3 0-0 is good for Black. He continues in pretty fashion: 10 cxb4 Nxc4 11 Qxc4 Rc8 12 Qf4 Re8† 13 Ne2 (13 Be3 Rc1† 14 Kd2 Bg4† 15 Qd4 Rd1†) 13...Rxe2†! 14 Kxe2 Bb5† 15 Ke1 Qe8† 16 Be3 Rc1† 17 Kd2 Rxh1 — +.

6 ....   e5
7 d3

Overly greedy is 7 Ng5 Bc5 8 Bxf7† (8 Nxf7 Bxf2† 9 Kxf2 Qb6† 10 Ke1 Bg4) 8...Ke7 9 Bc4 Bxf2† 10 Kxf2 Bg4 11 Be2 Qd4† 12 Kf1 Ne4 13 Nxe4 Rhf8† 14 Bf3 Qxe4 15 Qe2 Bxf3 − + Buzek − Kolozeiczik, 1958.

7	Bc5
8 Nc3	

8 0-0 Bg4 9 h3 Bh5 10 Bg5 (10 Be3 Bxe3 11 fxe3 Qb6 12 Qc1 0-0-0 ∞) 10...h6 11 Bxf6 Qxf6 12 g4 Bg6 13 Nc3 0-0-0 14 Qe2 may be a little better for White, but Black is not without counterplay.

8	Bg4
9 h3	Bh5
10 Bg5	

Now 10...h6 11 Bxf6 Qxf6 12 Ne4 Qe7 13 Nxc5 Qxc5 14 g4 Bg6 15 Qe2 followed by 0-0-0 is clearly better for White therefore the position after 10 Bg5 offers Black insufficient compensation for his pawn.

C3b.

4	b5

A sharp and interesting move which seems to fall short of equality.

5 Bb3

5 Be2 is considered best by many books . . . White tries to play as in C2. hoping that Black's pawn on b5 will prove weakening. Black's idea is to use his b5 pawn to help control the important d5 square by making a c2-c4 advance more difficult for White. Play usually continues 5...Nxd5 6 d4 (6 Bf3 Bc6 7 Ne2 Nf6 8 Bxc6† Nxc6 9 0-0 e6 10 d4 Be7 11 Qd3 Nb4 12 Qd1 0-0 = Suetin − Bronstein, USSR 1965) 6...e6 7 Nf3 Bd6 (7...c5?! is unwise: 8 0-0 Qb6 9 c4 bxc4 10 Bxc4 Be7 11 Re1 Nc7 12 d5 led to only trouble for Black in Voronov − Mikenas, Leningrad 1971; a new idea though is to play 7...Be7 with the idea of meeting 8 0-0 0-0 9 a4 with 9...bxa4! 10 c4 Nb6 when 11 Ne5 can be met with 11...Nc6!? 12 Bf3 Nxe5 sacrificing an exchange, or by 11...Be8!? 12 Bf3 f6! 13 Bxa8 fxe5 which looks quite promising.) 8 0-0 0-0 (8...Bc6?! led to a White advantage in Matulovic − Bronstein, Hamburg 1965 after 9 a4 b4 10 c4 bxc3 11 bxc3 0-0 12 c4 Nf4 13 Bxf4 Bxf4 14 Nc3 Qf6 15 Bd3 Nd7 16 Be4.) Now Schwarz gives 9 Ne5 Bxe5 10 dxe5 Nc6 11 Bxb5 (I suppose he intends to answer 11 f4 with 11...Qb8! with the idea of 12...Qb6† and placing a rook on d8) 11...Nxe5 12 Be2 c5 13 c4 Nb6 14 Na3 Qf6 ∓. 9 a4!? seems more critical, though a timely c7-c5 (e.g. 9...bxa4 10 c4 Nb4 11 Nc3 c5 or 9...b4 10 c4 bxc3 11 bxc3 c5) should give Black a reasonable game. It seems that 5 Be2 is not as fearsome as many authors make it out to be.

5	Bg4

5...a5 6 a4 b4 7 c4 favors White, as does 5...Bf5 6 Qe2 a6 7 a4! b4 8 c4 c6 9 d4 cxd5 10 c5!.

6 f3

It is possible that 6 Nf3!? is stronger. After 6...Nxd5 7 Nc3 Nxc3 White has two possibilities: i. 8 bxc3 (8 Bxf7†?? Kxf7 9 Ne5† Kg8! 10 Qxg4 Qd5 fails utterly for White) 8...e6 9 h3 Bh5 (9...Bxf3 10 Qxf3 Nd7 11 a4! b4 12 a5! bxc3 13 Ba4! Rb8 14 Qg3 leaves Black completely tied up.) 10 Qe2 Nd7 (10...a6 11 a4!) 11 g4 Bg6 12 Qxb5 Be4 13 Qe2 Nc5? (13...Bb7 is better, though White's game is still preferable.) 14 d4 Qf6 (14...Nxb3 15 Qxe4 Nxa1 16 Qc6† Ke7 17 Ba3† Kf6 18 g5† Kf5 19 Rg1 when the threat of Nh4† is decisive.) 15 Ba4†! c6 (15...Nxa4 16 Qxe4 Nb6 17 Qxc6† Kd8 18 Bg5) 16 Qxe4! Nxe4 17 Bxc6† Kd8 18 Bxe4 wins for White due to the double threat of 19 Bxa8 and 19 Bg5.

ii. 8 Ne5!? A fun move to play! 8...Qd4 9 Qxg4 Qxe5† 10 Kf1 f5 11 Qf3 Ne4 12 d3 c5! (12...Nc6 13 dxe4 Nd4 14 Qc3 is good for White) 13 dxe4 c4 14 exf5 Qd6! 15 Qh5† Kd8 (15...g6 16 fxg6 threatens Qxb5†) 16 Be3 Kc7 17 Rd1 Qc6 18 Bf4† Kb7 19 h4! White's rook will come into play via h3. White has good chances for his piece . . . Perhaps ∞ is a safe way out.

| 6 | .... | | Bc8 |
| 7 | Nc3! | | |

Holding on to the pawn by 7 a4 b4 8 c4? (8 Ne2! Nxd5 9 c4 Nf6 10 d4 a5 11 0-0 e6 12 Be3 led to a slight edge for White in Shuravliev — Hribosek, correspondence 1966) led to a quick demise in Seppelt — Schmeil: 8...c6 9 dxc6 Nxc6 10 Ne2 e5 11 0-0 Bc5† 12 Kh1 Bf5 13 Bc2 Bd3! 14 b3 h5! 15 Bb2 h4! 16 Bxd3 Qxd3 17 Nc1 Nh5! 18 g4 Ng3† 19 hxg3 hxg3† 20 Kg2 Rh2† 21 Kxg3 Qh7! 22 Bxe5 g5! 0 - 1.

Also offering little is 7 Ne2 Nxd5 (7...Bb7?! 8 Nbc3 a6 9 d4 Nbd7 10 Bg5 h6 11 Bh4 ± Sellos — Belbin, Buenos Aires 1978) 8 d4 e6 9 Nbc3 (9 0-0 Be7 10 a4 b4 11 c4 bxc3 12 bxc3 a5 13 Na3 0-0 ,14 Nc2 Ba6 15 c4? Nb6 16 Ne3 c5 17 Bb2 Nc6 left Black with an excellent position, Zatulowskaja — Mosiontschik, 1963) 9...Nxc3 10 Nxc3 a6 11 Be3 Be7 12 0-0 0-0 13 d5? c5 14 dxc6 Nxc6 15 a4 b4 16 Ne4 Qc7 17 Qe2 Na5 Black has the edge. Fuderer — Pfeiffer, 1950.

Logical, but leading to no advantage, is 7 Qe2 a6 8 Nc3 (8 a4 b4 9 Qc4 Qd6 10 d3 e6 11 Bf4 e5 12 Bg5 Bb7 led to an unclear struggle, Keres — Lutikov, Tallinn 1964) 8...Nbd7 9 Ne4 Nb6 10 Nxf6† gxf6 11 Qe4 Bb7 12 Ne2 e6 13 Nf4 Bd6 11 d3 Qe7 15 Bd2 f5 16 Qe2 e5 17 Nh3 Nxd5 18 0-0-0 0-0-0 19 g3 c5 Black had a powerful bind and went on to win in Barishev — Pavlenko, USSR 1980.

| 7 | .... | | b4 |
| 8 | Ne4 | | Nxd5 |

9 d4 e6 10 Ne2 Be7 11 0-0 0-0 12 c4 Nb6 13 Be3 Nc6 14 Qd3 Ba6 15 Bc2 f5 16 b3!

White's position is clearly superior. Sellos — Haas, Berne 1979.

C3c.

4 ....   Bg4!

This offers Black good chances.

5 f3

Diagram 37   After 4...Bg4

C3c1. 5...Bc8; C3c2. 5...Bf5.

C3c1.

5 ....   Bc8

This seems inferior to 5...Bf5 as White is no longer forced into weakening his kingside by g2-g4.

6 Nc3   Nbd7
7 d4

Simple and good. Many alternatives have been tried:

i. 7 Qe2?! Nb6 (7...a6 8 a4 Nb6 9 Qd3 g6 10 g4 Bg7 11 Nge2 h5! 12 g5 Nfd7 13 f4 Nc5 14 Qe3 Ncxa4! 15 Bb3 Nxc3 16 Nxc3 0-0 17 0-0 c6 18 Qf3 Bg4 19 Qg2 cxd5 20 Nxd5 Be6   0 - 1 Paar — Bozic, Beverwijk 1968, since 21 Nxb6 Qxb6† 22 Kh1 Bxb3 23 cxb3 e6! leaves White's position shattered.) 8 Qd3 g6 9 Nge2 Bg7. 10 Ng3 0-0 11 b3 a6 12 0-0 Nxc4 13 bxc4 b5! 14 Rb1 bxc4 15 Qxc4 e6! 16 dxe6 Bxe6 17 Qa4 Nd5 Black has excellent compensation for his pawn, Belov — Zilin, USSR 1961.

ii. 7 d3 leads to nothing after 7...Nb6 8 Nge2 Nfxd5 Nxd5 9 Nxd5 10 0-0 g6 11 Ng3 Bg7 12 f4 e6 13 Qf3 c6 14 c3 0-0 Muchin-Boleslavski, USSR '64.

iii. 7 Nge2 can often transpose into 7 d4. On a more independent basis: 7 Nge2 Nb6 8 Bb3 Nbxd5 9 d4 Nxc3 (9...e6? 10 Ne4! Be7 11 c4 Nb6 12 0-0 0-0 13 Be3 is clearly better for White, Hultquist — Balogh, Corr. 1968) 10 Nxc3 e6 11 0-0 a5 (11...Be7 12 Ne4 0-0 13 c4 $\pm$) 12 a3 Be7 13 Ne4 a4 14 Ba2 0-0 15 c4 Nxe4 16 fxe4 e5! should be fine for Black, e.g. 17 dxe5 (17 d5 Bc5† 18 Kh1 Qh4; 17 Be3 Bg5!) 17...Qxd1! (less clear is 17...Bc5† 18 Kh1 Qxd1 19 Rxd1 Bg4 20 Rd5! b6 21 h3 when 21...c6? 22 Rxc5! Bd7 23 e6! loses and 21...Be6 22 Rd1 Rad8 23 Bg5 favors White) 18 Rxd1 Bg4! 19 Rd3 Bc5† (19...Rad8 20 Rxd8 Bc5†! is also fine) 20 Be3 Bxe3† 21 Rxe3 and now 21...Ra5, 21...Rfe8, or even 21...Rad8.

iv. **7 Ne4!?** An important move, highly thought of by theory. 7...Nb6
8 Nxf6† gxf6 9 Bb3 Nxd5 10 d4 Rg8 (10...Bf5?! 11 g4! Bg6 12 Ne2! with
the idea of 13 c4 Nb4 14 Nf4 is good for White but 10...h5!? 11 c4 Nb6
12 Qd3 c5 13 d5 e5 is interesting.) 11 g3 c6 12 Qd3 f5 13 Bd2 e6 14 0-0-0
a5 15 Kb1 Niephaus — Thorbergsson, 1956 is considered good for White, but
is 15...a4 16 Bxd5 cxd5 really so bad?

	7	Nb6
	8 Bb3	

Insipid is 8 Bb5† Bd7 9 Bd3 Nbxd5 10 Nxd5 Nxd5 11 a3 (11 Ne2 c5!
Znapik — Gipslis, Lublin 1972) 11...b5 12 Ne2 e6 13 0-0 Bd6 = Matev —
Valkesalmi, Groningen 1978/79.

	8	Nbxd5
	9 Nxd5	Nxd5
	10 c4	Nf6
	11 Be3	

11 Ne2 is similar. A game Guldin — Chalibeili, 1963, saw White try queen-
side castling which led to a nice Black victory: 11 Ne2 g6 12 Bg5 Bg7 13
Qd2 h6 14 Be3 c6 15 0-0-0?! a5 16 Nc3 b5 17 cxb5 cxb5 18 Nxb5 a4 19
Bc4 Ba6 20 Kb1 Qd7 21 Na3 Nd5 22 Bxd5 Qxd5 23 Rc1 h5 24 Rc5 Qd7
25 Nc4 Bxc4 26 Rxc4 0-0 27 Rhc1 Rfb8 28 Rc7 Qf5† 29 Qc2 Qe6 30
Qe4? a3 31 R1c2? Qxa2†! 0-1.

	11	c6
	12 Qd2	g6
	13 Ne2	Bg7
	14 0-0	0-0
	15 Rad1	b5!

A typical idea in this variation.

	16 cxb5	cxb5
	17 d5	a5
	18 a3	Ba6
	19 Rfe1	Qd7

19...a4 20 Ba2 Qd6!?

	20 Qxa5!	

Alexandria — Gaprindashvili, Picunda-Tibilisi 1975 continued less accurately: 20 Kh1 a4 21 Ba2 Rfc8 22 Bd4 b4! 23 axb4 (23 Qxb4 Bxe2 24 Rxe2
Nxd5 25 Qd2 Bxd4 26 Qxd4 e6! =) 23...Bc4 24 Bxc4 Rxc4 25 Bc5 Qf5!
26 Nc3 (26 Ng3 Qxd5 27 Qxd5 Nxd5 28 Rxd5 Bxb2!) 26...Nd7 27 Bxe7
a3! 28 Re4 Rxe4 29 fxe4 Qe5 30 Qg5 axb2! 31 Qxe5 Bxe5 32 Nb1 f6
33 b5 Rb8 34 Na3 Rc8! 35 Bb4 Rc1 36 Re1 Bd6! 37 Bd2 Rxe1† 38 Bxe1
Bxa3 0-1.

	20	b4
	21 Ba4!	Bxe2

21...Qd6 22 Bc6!.

22 Qxa8 Rxa8 23 Bxd7 Bxd1 24 Bc6 Ra6 25 Rxd1 bxa3 26 bxa3 Rxa3 27 Bc5 + — .

C3c2.

5	Bf5

C3c2a. 6 Ne2; C3c2b. 6 c3; C3c2c. 6 g4; C3c2d. 6 Nc3.

C3c2a.

6 Ne2	

The start of an aggressive, but rather lame system.

6	Nxd5
7 Ng3	

7 d4 e6 8 Ng3 Bg6 9 0-0 Nc6 10 c3 Qd7 11 Ne4 0-0-0 gives Black fine play, Weglows — Witkowski, Poland 1975.

7	Bg6
8 0-0	e6
9 f4	Nc6

9...Nb6?! 10 Bb3 Bc5† 11 Kh1 0-0 12 Nc3 Nc6 13 Nce4 led to a small edge for White in Mieses — Marshall, Karlovy Vary 1907. A good alternative to 9...Nc6 though is 9...Ne7 10 d4 h5, a suggestion of Rabar's which looks quite attractive.

10 d4	Nce7

Bad is 10...h5 11 c3 h4? 12 f5 hxg3 13 fxg6 gxh2† (13...Rxh2 14 gxf7† Kd7 15 Qg4 Qh4 16 Qxh4 Rxh4 17 Bxd5 exd5 18 Bf4! with advantage to White.) 14 Kh1 f6 15 Re1 Qd6 16 Qg4 Kd7 17 b4 Nce7 18 Nd2 f5 19 Qg5 Qf4 20 Nf3 Qxg5 21 Ne5†! Black is badly tied up. Gresser — Wolpert, 1959; playable, however, is 10...Nde7 11 c3 h5 12 Qe2 Qd7 13 Nd2 0-0-0 14 Nf3 h4 15 Ne4 Nf5 16 Neg5 Bd6 17 Bb5 with just a slight initiative for White in O. Smith — Bergraser, correspondence 1960 (eventually drawn).

11 Bb3	h5
12 Qe2	h4
13 Ne4	Bxe4
14 Qxe4	Nf5
15 c3	Be7
16 Nd2	c5
17 Nf3	

Not 17 dxc5?? Bxc5† 18 Kh1 Ng3†.

17	cxd4
18 Ba4†	Kf8

Schmid — Bergraser, correspondence 1955. Black has a good position.

C3c2b.

6 c3	

A solid little move which gives White nothing.

6	a6!

Hans Müller's move. Alternatives are not as good: 6...Nxd5? 7 Qb3 is very bad for Black; 6...Nbd7 7 g4 Bg6 (7...Nb6?? 8 gxf5 Nxc4 9 Qa4†) 8 g5 Nh5 9 d4 ±.

	7 a4!	

7 g4 Bxb1 8 Rxb1 b5 9 Bb3 Nxd5 =.

	7	Nbd7
	8 a5	Ne5
	9 d4	Nxc4
	10 Qa4†	Qd7
	11 Qxc4	Qxd5
	12 Qxd5	

12 Qxc7 is very risky, after 12...Rc8 13 Qe5 Qxe5 14 dxe5 Nd7 15 f4 Nc5 leads to a powerful initiative for Black. Black can also force a draw by 12...Bxb1 13 Rxb1 Qa2 14 Qxb7 Rd8 15 Qc6† Rd7 (15...Nd7? 16 Qe4) 16 Qc8† Rd8 17 Qc6† with a perpetual check.

	12	Nxd5
	13 Na3 =.	

C3c2c.

6 g4

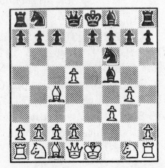

Diagram 38   After 6 g4

A critical move. Though it forces Black's bishop back and gains space it also weakens White's kingside.

	6	Bc8!

6...Bg6? is known to be bad: 7 Nc3 c6 (7...Nbd7 8 g5 Nb6 9 Bb5† Nfd7 10 d4 a6 11 Bd3 Nb8 12 Be4 +−)8 f4! (8 dxc6? Nxc6 9 Nge2 Qb6 10 g5 Ne5! 11 Bb5† Nfd7 12 Nf4 0-0-0 Suetin — Korchnoi, 1960. Black has an active game.) 8...h5 9 f5 Bh7 10 g5 Nxd5 11 Qxh5 Qd7 12 g6 fxg6 13 fxg6 Qe6† 14 Nge2 Qxg6 15 Qxg6 Bxg6 16 Nxd5 cxd5 17 Bxd5 +− Shagalovich — Veresov, USSR 1961.

	7 Nc3	c6!?

Other moves are also possible:

i. 7...Nbd7, see game # 7;

ii. 7...a6 8 g5! (8 a4 c6! [or 8...Nbd7 9 Ba2 Nb6 10 Nge2 Nbxd5 11 g5
Nxc3 12 Nxc3 Nh5 13 d4 g6 14 Be3 Bg7 ∞ Suetin — Mikenas, USSR '64]
9 dxc6 Nxc6 10 d3 e5 11 Be3 Nd4 12 Nce2 Bc5 [12...h5! 13 g5 Nd5!
looks good] 13 Nxd4 Bxd4 [13...exd4 14 Bd2 0-0 15 Ne2 Nxg4 16 fxg4
Qh4† 17 Ng3 Bxg4 18 Qc1 Re8† is an interesting suggestion by Gipslis]
14 Bxd4 Qxd4 15 c3 Qc5 16 Qe2 0-0 17 Nh3 Bd7 18 a5 Rac8 19 Nf2 Nd5
20 Ne4 Qc6 21 Bxd5 Qxd5 Black has adequate compensation for the pawn.
Alexandria — Gaprindashvili, Tibilisi 1975) 8...b5 9 Bb3 Nfd7 10 d4 Nb6
11 Nge2 b4 (Gipslis gives 11...Bb7 12 Nf4 b4 as unclear but 13 Na4 still
seems at least ±) 12 Na4 Nxd5 13 Qd3 e6 14 Bd2 Be7 15 h4 Nd7 16 0-0-0
Bb7 17 Rdg1 0-0 18 h5 White has a clear advantage. Alexandria — Gaprindashvili, Tibilisi 1975.

8	dxc6	Nxc6
9	d3	e5
10	g5	Nh5
11	Ne4	Be7
12	Nge2	0-0
13	Be3	

13 c3?! turned out badly in Alexandria — Gaprindashvili, Tibilisi 1975
after 13...Na5 14 Be3 Nxc4 15 dxc4 Qc7 16 b3 Bh3 17 Rg1 Rad8 18 Qc2
Kh8 19 Rd1 (19 Bd2!?) 19...Rxd1† 20 Kxd1 Qd7†! 21 Kc1 Qf5 22 Nd2
Ba3† 23 Kb1 Rd8 24 Ng3 Nxg3 25 Rxg3? (25 hxg3 Bc5! 26 Bxc5 Rd2
27 Qxf5 Bxf5† 28 Ka1 b6 is clearly an improvement though I still prefer
Black.) 25...b6! 26 Rg1 Bc5! 27 Bxc5 Rxd2 28 Qxf5 Bxf5† 29 Kc1 Rc2†
— + .

13	....	Na5

13...Nd4 14 Bxd4 exd4 15 Qd2.

14	Bb3	Nxb3
15	axb3	f5
16	gxf6	

16 Ne4-g3?! Bxg5!

16	....	Bxf6

with Bh4 to come. Black has full compensation for his pawn.

C3c2d.
6 Nc3
The main line in the 3 Bb5† variation.

6	....	Nbd7

Unsound is 6...c6 7 dxc6 Nxc6 8 d3 e5 9 Be3! ± Larsen.
7 Qe2
Other moves did not lead to a tangible advantage for White:

i. 7 Nge2 Nb6 8 Bb3 (8 b3 g6 9 Ng3 Bg7 10 Nxf5 gxf5 11 Bb5† Kf8
12 Bb2 Nfxd5 = Korelov — Resko, USSR 1960) 8...Nbxd5 9 Nxd5 (9 d4

Nxc3 10 Nxc3 a5 11 a4 e6 12 0-0 Bd6 13 Ne4 0-0 14 Nxd6 cxd6 15 c3
d5 = Plater — Karaklaic, 1956) 9...Nxd5 10 d4 (10 Ng3 Bg6 11 0-0 e6 12 f4
Ne7 13 d4 h5! 14 Re1 h4 15 Ne4 Bxe4 16 Rxe4 Nf5 17 c3 Qd6 18 Qe1
0-0-0 ∓ Ciric — Tot, Yugoslavia 1956) 10...e6 11 0-0 Be7 12 Kh1 (12 c4)
12...0-0 13 c4 Nb6 (13...Nf6! with c6 & b5 seems better) 14 Be3 ± Jezek —
Tesar, 1962;

ii. 7 d3 Nb6 8 Nge2 Nbxd5 9 Nxd5 Nxd5 10 Ng3 g6! (or 10...Qd7 11
0-0 h5 12 d4 0-0-0 ∞ Spaski — Banks, Canada 1971; 10...Bg6 11 f4 e6 12
0-0 Nb6?! 13 Bb3 Bc5† 14 Kh1 0-0 15 Qf3 Qc8 16 Ne2 Nd7 17 g4 led to
a White advantage in Maroczy — Menchik, 1929 but 12...Ne7! & 13...h5
should be fine.) 11 f4 Qd6 12 Qf3 0-0-0 13 Nxf5 gxf5 14 Bxd5? Qxd5 15
Qxd5 Rxd5 ∓ Fichtl — Karaklaid, 1957;

iii. 7 d4 Nb6 8 Bb5† Bd7 9 Bd3 Nbxd5 10 Ne4! e6 11 c3 Bc6 12 Ne2
Qd7 13 0-0 0-0-0 ∞ ;

iv. 7 g4?! Nb6 8 Qe2 Bc8 (8...Bxc2?? 9 Bb5† & d3) 9 Qd3 g6 (Schwarz
mentions 9...Nxc4 10 Qxc4 a6 11 a4 a6 12 dxe6 Bxe6) 10 b3 Bg7 11 Bb2
0-0 12 0-0-0 a6 13 Nge2 Nxc4 14 bxc4 b5! 15 Ne4 bxc4 16 Nxf6† Bxf6
17 Qxc4 Rb8 18 Bxf6 exf6 19 Nc3 Qd6 20 Rde1 Bd7 21 h4 Rb4 Black
had excelletn attacking prospects. Aronin — Schamkovich, USSR 1959.

7	Nb6
8 Bb3	Qd7

Black can't regain his pawn by 8...Nfxd5? 9 Nxd5 Nxd5 10 Qb5† c6 11
Qxb7 so he prepares the capture by the logical 8...Qd7. A game Malesic —
Karaklaic, 1966 saw Black prepare the capture by 8...a6? but he ended up in
trouble after 9 Qe5! Qd7 10 g4 Bg6 11 Nge2 h6 12 d3 0-0-0 13 Bf4.

9 d6

9 d3 or 9 d4 Nfxd5 should give Black a comfortable game.

9	Qxd6

The only correct move. 9...cxd6? 10 a4 a5 11 d3 Be6 (11...d5? 12 Qe5
e6 13 Nb5 Rc8 14 Bd2 is very bad.) 12 Bxe6 Qxe6 13 Qxe6 fxe6 14 Nb5
Kd7 15 c4! d5 16 Be3 Nc8 17 Bd4! leaves Black in sad shape. While 9...c6?
10 dxe7 Bxe7 11 d3 0-0 12 Qf2 c5 13 Nge2 Rac8 14 0-0 c4 15 dxc4 Nxc4
16 Bxc4 Rxc4 17 Rd1 Qc8 18 Be3 a6 19 Rd2 Cholmov — Goldenov, USSR
1961, leaves Black with insufficient compensation for the pawn.

10 Nb5	Qd7
11 Qe5	0-0-0!
12 Nxa7†	

12 Nxc7? Qxc7 13 Qxf5† e6 14 Qa5 Bc5 15 Qxa7 Qe5† 16 Ne2 Kc7!
17 Qa5 Bf2† — + .

12	Kb8
13 Nb5	Nfd5
14 a4	

14 Nd4? e6 15 d3 (15 Nxf5 exf5 16 Ne2 Bc5 17 Qxg7 Rhe8!) 15...Bxd3! 16 Bd2 (16 cxd3 Nb4 17 Qe3 Qxd4 18 Qxd4 Rxd4) 16...Nb4! 17 0-0-0 (17 Bxb4 Bxb4† 18 c3 Qxd4) 17...Bxc2 18 Bxc2 (18 Nxc2? Nd3† 0 - 1, Smejkal — Jaros, 1963) 18...Nc4! 19 Qe4 f5 20 Qe2 Qxd4 21 Bc3 Nxa2† 22 Kb1 Nxc3† 23 bxc3 Qb6†.

| 14 .... | f6! |

This leads to a very strong position for Black. Jack Peter's recommendation of 14...e6 gives Black good play after 15 d3 (15 Ne2? f6 16 Qd4 e5 17 Qf2 Nb4 18 d3 Bxd3; 15 d4?! f6 16 Qe2 e5 allows Black to break open the position; 15 Qe2 Nb4 16 d3 e5 gives Black plenty of play. Note that 15 Qe2 Nb4 16 d4? e5! 17 dxe5 Bc5 18 a5? Nc4! is catastrophic.) 15...f6 16 Qe2 (16 Qd4 e5 17 Qf2 Nb4) 16...e5. Analysis of 14...e6 by J. Peters.

| 15 Qe2 | e5 |

15...Nf4? 16 Qf2 e5 17 Ne2 Nxe2 18 Qxe2 Bc5 19 d3 Rhe8 20 Nc3 Bg6 21 Be3 Bd4 22 0-0 + —Shagalovich — Rojzman, USSR 1961.

| 16 a5 | Nf4 |

16...Nc8 17 a6.

17 axb6	Nxe2
18 bxc7†	Qxc7
19 Nxc7	Nd4
20 Na8	Bxc2!

Diagram 39

After 20...Bxc2

Almost all books give 20...Bc5 here, saying that 'Black will win White's knight by 21...Nc6 & Ba7 after which his active pieces will give him an edge.' This seems hard to believe! For instance 21 Ne2 Nc6 22 d3 Ba7 23 Rxa7! frees White's knight and leaves White with a decisive material advantage. Also 22...Na7 23 Ng3 Bg6 24 Ne4 Bxe4 25 fxe4 Kxa8 26 Ke2 Kb8 27 Be3 Bxe3 28 Kxe3 leaves White a solid pawn up. The improvement 20...Bxc2! though is clearly favorable to Black.

| 21 Ba4 |

White has many tries:

i. 21 Ba2? Kxa8; ii. 21 Bf7 Bc5! threatens 22...Ba7 **23** Rxa7 Kxa7

24 Nc7 Rd7; iii. 21 Bc4 b5 22 Be2 Nb3 ∓.

| | 21 .... | b5 |
| | 22 Bxb5 | |

22 Nb6 is no better.

| | 22 .... | Nxb5 |
| | 23 Nb6 | |

Black threatens 23...Kb7.

| | 23 .... | Bb3! |

Now Black threatens 24...Rd6 25 Na4 Ra6 and 24 Ne2 Rd6 25 Na4 Ra6 26 Nec3 Nxc3 is certainly no help.

| | 24 d3 | |

24 Na4 Nd4!

| | 24 .... | Rxd3 |

Not 24...Bb4†? 25 Bd2 Bxd2† 26 Kxd2 Rd6? 27 Ra8†.

	25 Bd2	Kb7
	26 Na4	Nd4!
	27 Nh3!	Be7!

27...Nc2† 28 Ke2 Bc4 29 Rac1!

| | 28 Nf2 | |

28 Nc3 Rhd8! − +.

	28	Nc2†
	29 Ke2	Rxd2†
	30 Kxd2	Nxa1
	31 Rxa1	Ra8 − +.

Chapter Three

1 e4	d5
2 exd5	Nf6
3 d4	

Diagram 40   After 3 d4

White's simplest and strongest method; he simply ignores the pawn and goes about building a strong center.

| 3 .... | Nxd5 |

3...g6 4 c4 b5 can hardly be good: 5 c5 (5 b3 Bg7 6 Nf3 0-0 7 Be2 c6 8 dxc6 bxc4 9 bxc4 Nxc6 and now not 10 0-0? Ne4! 11 Be3 f5! with good play for Black, but instead 10 Nc3 with advantage to White) 5...Nxd5 (5...a6!? 6 a4 b4 7 Bc4 Nxd5 8 Qb3) 6 Bxb5† c6 7 Be2 Bg7 8 Nf3 0-0 9 0-0 Na6 10 Nc3 Rb8 11 Nxd5 Qxd5 12 b3 Nxc5 13 Bf4! Rb4 14 Bd2 Rxd4 15 Nxd4 Bxd4 16 Rac1 Rd8 17 Be3 Ne6 18 Bc4 White was winning. Stoltz — Richter, Zappot 1935.

A. 4 Nf3; B. 4 c4.

A.

4 Nf3

As this and 4 c4 often transpose, here we will only consider lines in which White avoids c2-c4.

4 ....   Bg4

i. 4...Bf5 5 Bd3 (5 Be2 is Chapter Two, C2b.; 5 a3 led to an advantage for White after 5...e6 6 c4 Nb6 7 Nc3 Be7 8 Qb3 Qc8 9 c5 Nb6-d7 10 Bf4 Nf6 11 Bc4 c6 12 0-0 Nd5 13 Bxd5 exd5 14 Rae1 Be6 15 Bg5. Bronstein — Shamkovic, USSR 1961; for 5 c3 see game # 8) 5...Bxd3 (5...Bg6 6 Ne5 e6 7 g3 ±) 6 Qxd3 Nc6?! (6...e6 is better, when 7 Qb5†? Nc6 8 Qxb7?? Ndb4 wins for Black) 7 c4 Ndb4 8 Qb3 e5 9 0-0! Nxd4 (9...exd4 10 a3!) 10 Nxd4 Qxd4 11 Nc3 Qb6 (11...0-0-0? 12 Rd1 Nd3 13 Be3 Qg4 14 Nb5) 12 c5! Qxc5 (12...Bxc5 13 Na4) 13 a3 Nd3 14 Qxb7 Rd8 15 Be3 Qc4 16 Nb5 Bd6 17 b3 Qe6 18 Qc6† Ke7! (18...Qd7? 19 Nxd6† cxd6 20 Qc3 Nc5 21 Bxc5) Tal — Korchnoi, USSR 1961, and now 19 Nxa7 would have given White a clear advantage.;

ii. 4...g6 5 Be2 Bg7 6 0-0 0-0 7 h3 Nc6 (7...c6 8 Re1 Nd7 9 Bf1 Re8 10 c4 Nc7 11 Nc3 with advantage in Geller — Maric, Skopje-Obrid 1968) 8 Re1 (9 c4 Nb6 9 d5 Ne5 10 Nxe5 Bxe5 11 Nc3 e6 12 Re1 Bg7 13 Bf4 exd5 14 c5 White is better. Geller — Wade, 1965. Perhaps Black should try 9...Na5!?) 8...Nb6 9 c3 a5!? 10 Na3 a4 11 Bb5 Bd7 12 Bg5 Re8 13 Qe2 Qc8 14 Rad1 Na5 15 Bd3 Bf5 16 Bf4 c6 17 Ne5 Nd5 18 Bc1 White stands better. Sigurleijohsson — Tuzhovsky, Tbilisi 1974.

5 Be2

Sharper is 5 h3 Bh5 (5...Bxf3!? 6 Qxf3 c6 followed by g6 & Bg7 would lead to a solid position for Black.) 6 g4 (6 c4!? Nb6 7 Qb3! Bxf3 8 Qxf3 Qxd4 9 Qxb7 e5 10 Nc3 Kapengut — Shereshevsky, Minsk 1978 seems like a promising method of play for White. Perhaps 8...c6!? followed by g6 & Bg7.) 6...Bg6 7 Ne5 Nc6 (7...Nd7 8 Nxg6 hxg6 9 Bg2 c6 10 c4 N5b6 11 Qe2 Nf6 12 Be3 e6 13 Nc3 favors White. Razuvaiev — Gipslis, USSR 1973.) 8 Nxg6 (A game between Alexandria — Gaprindashvili, Tibilisi 1975 reached a position with mutual chances after 8 Nxc6 bxc6 9 Bg2 Qd6 10 Na3 h5 11 g5 Qe6† 12 Qe2 Qxe2† 13 Kxe2 0-0-0 14 c4 Nb4) 8...hxg6 9 Bg2 Qd6 (9...e6 10 c4 Bb4†? 11 Ke2! Nde7 12 d5 or 11...Nb6 12 Bxc6† bxc6

71

13 c5 both will leave White a piece ahead.) 10 Nc3 Nf4 11 Bxf4 Qxf4 12 Qd3 (12 Ne2!? Qd6 13 Qd2 0-0-0 14 0-0-0 ±) 12...0-0-0 13 Bxc6 (13 Ne2!? Qd6 14 0-0-0) 13...bxc6 14 Ne2 Qg5 (14...Qxg4!? 15 hxg4 Rxh1† 16 Kd2 Rxa1 is interesting but should favor White due to Black's weak pawns and disconnected rooks.) 15 Qc4! Timoshenko — Gipslis, Leningrad 1975, White is better, e.g. 15...Qd5 16 Qa6† Kb8 17 0-0-0 e6 (17...Qb5 18 Qxb5 cxb5 19 d5! favors White) 18 c4 Qf3 19 d5! cxd5 (19...Qxe2 20 dxc6 + —) 20 Nd4 + —.

5 .... e6

6 0-0

6 h3 Bh5 (6...Bxf3 is playable: 7 Bxf3 c6 8 0-0 Bd6 9 c4 Ne7 10 Nc3 0-0 11 Ne2 Nd7 12 b3 Nf5 Andric — Karaklaic, Yugoslavia 1951 and now 13 g3 is ±) 7 0-0 Be7?! (7...Nc6 is correct; see Chapter 3, B3b2b.) 8 c4 (also good is 8 Ne5 Bxe2 9 Qxe2 0-0 10 c4 Nf6 11 Rd1 Nc6 12 Be3! Nxe5 13 dxe5 Nd7 14 Nc3 Qc8 15 f4 ±) 8...Nb6 9 Be3 Nc6 10 Nbd2 0-0 11 Rc1 ± Van Wijgerden — Christiansen, IBM 2 1978. Black should generally play ...Nc6 before ...Be7 since in many lines the exchange won't be threatened (by Bxb7) after White plays c2-c4 and Black replies with Nb6 & Bxf3. In that case Black can often safely capture on c4, see note to 7...Be7?!.; 6 c3 is a bit passive. Black should avoid the premature 6...c5 7 Nbd2 Nc6 8 Nb3 cxd4 9 Nbxd4 with advantage to White. (A game Cardose — Phillippe, 1961 continued 9...Nxd4? 10 Qxd4 Bxf3 11 Qa4†! Ke7 12 Bxf3 f6 13 0-0 Kf7 14 Rd1 and Black soon resigned.). After 6 c3 better is 6...Nc6 or 6...Nd7 (see game # 9.).

6 .... Nc6

6...Be7?! 7 h3 transposes into the last note; while 6...Bd6? 7 c4 Nf4 8 c5 Nxe2† 9 Qxe2 Be7 10 Qb5† is unplayable for Black; similar to the Caro-Kan Kann is the super solid 6...c6, a move used with success by Capablanca! His play was quite instructive: 7 c4 Nf6 8 Nc3 Nbd7 9 h3 (9 d5 Bb4! 10 dxc6 bxc6 11 Qa4 Bxc3 12 bxc3 0-0! 13 Qxc6 Rc8 14 Qa6 Nc5 15 Qa3 Nfe4 16 Be3 Rc6 17 Rfd1 Qc7 18 Bxc5 Rxc5 19 Rd4 Bxf3 20 Bxf3 Ra5 21 Qb2 Nc5 22 Rad1 Ra6 with more than enough compensation for the pawn, Michelsen — Capablanca, New York 1915.) 9...Bh5 10 Bf4 (10 d5 exd5 11 cxd5 Bb4) 10...Nb6 11 Qd3 Be7 12 Rad1 0-0 13 Ne5 Bxe2 14 Qxe2 Nc8! 15 Rd3 Qa5 16 a3? Nd6! 17 Bg5 Rad8 18 Rfd1 Qa6! 19 c5? (19 R3d2) 19...Nf5! 20 Qf3 (20 g4 Nd5!) 20...Nd5 21 Nxd5 Rxd5 22 Bxe7 Nxe7 23 Qe4 Ng6 24 f4 Rfd8 25 Kh2 Nxe5 26 fxe5 b6! 27 cxb6 axb6 28 Rg3 c5 29 Qh4 g6, Black won easily, Chajes — Capablanca, New York '15.

One gets the impression that Capablanca could have played any opening and won. There are several good methods to choose against 6...c6. One of the simplest is 7 c4 Nf6 8 Nc3 Nbd7 9 h3 Bh5 10 Be3 Be7 11 Ne5 Bxe2 (11...Nxe5 12 dxe5 Qxd1?? 13 Bxd1 wins a piece.) 12 Qxe2 Nxe5 13 dxe5

Nd7 14 f4 Vukovic — Popovic, Yugoslavia 1945, with a small but lasting advantage for White.

7 c3

7 c4! is B3b.; 7 h3 Bh5 8 c3 Be7 9 Ne5 Bxe2 (9...Nxe5 10 Bxh5 Ng6 11 Bf3 c6 12 Re1 0-0 13 Nd2 Qc7 14 Nc4 Rad8 15 Qe2 Bf6 = Vospernik — Karaklaic, Yugoslavia 1961) 10 Qxe2 Nxe5 11 dxe5 0-0 12 Rd1 Qb8 13 Rd3 Rd8 = Minic — Karaklaic, Yugoslavia 1962.

| 7 .... | Bd6 |

8 Ne5

8 Nbd2 Nf4 9 Ne4 Nxe2† 10 Qxe2 0-0 = 11 Bg5?! f6 12 Bh4 Qe8 13 h3 Bh5 14 Rfe1 e5! Black's game is preferable. Zinser — Karaklaic, Monte Carlo 1967.

8	Bxe2
9 Qxe2	Bxe5
10 dxe5	Qh4

Diagram 41

After 10...Qh4

The position is even. A game Duckstein — Bergraser, 1958 continued

11 Nd2

11 f4 0-0 = was Sikora — Commons, Lubin 1978.
11...Nf4 12 Qe4 Qg4 13 Kh1 Nxe5! 14 Nc4! Nfd3 15 Qxb7 Nxf2† 16 Kg1 Nh3† ½ - ½;

B.

4 c4

B1. 4...Nb4?!; B2. 4...Nf6; B3. 4...Nb6.

B1.

| 4 .... | Nb4?! |

(See diagram at top of next page)

A rather dubious move. White has only to avoid various tactical tricks.

5 a3

Also strong is 5 Qa4† N8c6 6 a3! (for 6 d5? see game # 10) 6...Na6 7 d5 (7 Be3 Bd7 8 Qc2 is also very good) 7...Nc5 8 Qd1 (8 Qb5? b6! 9 dxc6 a5 traps the queen, e.g. 10 b4 Ba6 11 bxc5 Bxb5 12 cxb5 Qd4 13 Ra2 Qe4†)

Diagram 42   After 4...Nb4

8...Ne5 9 b4 Ncd7 10 Bb2 Ng6 11 Nf3 Nf6 12 Bd3 ±.

                    5 ....   **N4c6**

5...N4a6 6 Nc3 g6 7 Be3 Bg7 8 Qd2 0-0 9 Nf3 c5 10 Rd1 Nc6 11 d5 ±
Medina — Sanz, Madrid 1943.

                    6 d5   **Ne5**
                    7 Nf3

A logical move, trading a knight which has moved once with one that has
moved (after the capture) six times! Also very good is 7 f4 Ng6 8 Bd3 e5 9
Qe2 Nd7 10 Nf3 Nc5 11 Nxe5 Nxe5 12 Qxe5† Be7 13 Bc2 0-0 14 0-0 Bg4
15 h3 Re8 16 hxg4 Nb3 17 Qxe7! Qxe7 18 Bxb3 Qh4 19 Bd2 Qxg4 20
Nc3 + −.

To be avoided, though, is 7 Bf4? Ng6 8 Bg3 e5! 9 dxe6 Qxd1† 10 Kxd1
Bxe6 11 Bxc7 Na6 12 Bg3 0-0-0† 13 Nd2 Nc5 14 Nf3 Nb3 15 Ra2 f5
Black had a strong initiative and eventually won in Klavin — Nei, USSR '58.

                    7 ....   **Nxf3†**

7...Bg4 8 Be2 Bxf3 9 Bxf3 is fine for White since 9...Nxc4?? fails to 10
Qa4†. Also possible is 8 Qb3!? Bxf3 9 gxf3.

                    8 Qxf3   **e5**

8...e6 9 Nc3 exd5 10 Nxd5 Bd6 (10...c6 11 Qe4† when 11...Be6 12 Nf4
and 11...Be7 12 Nxe7 are both nice for White.) 11 Be3 0-0 12 0-0-0.

                    9 Qg3!

9 dxe6 Bxe6 10 Qxb7 Nd7 gives Black unnecessary counterplay.

                    9 ....   **Nd7**
                    10 Bd3   **g6**
                    11 Nc3   **Bg7**
                    12 f4   **Nc5**
                    13 Bc2   **e4**
                    14 Nxe4   **Bf5**
                    15 Nxc5   **Bxc2**

16 Qe3† Kf8 Aratowski — Evdokimov, correspondence 1955, and now
17 0-0 leaves White with a huge advantage.

74

4 ....   Nf6

Diagram 43   After 4...Nf6

Black is not able to generate counterplay so easily after this and usually must be happy with a solid but passive game.

5 Nf3

Stops any stock sacrifices based on e7-e5 by Black. A famous example of this is Duras — Tartakower, Vienna 1908 which continued 5 Nc3 e5 6 dxe5 Qxd1† 7 Nxd1 Ng4 8 f4 Nc6 9 h3 Nh6 10 Ne3 Be6 11 Bd2 0-0-0 and here Schwarz gives the continuation as '12 Nf3 Nb4! ∓', but then 13 a3! Nd3† 14 Bxd3 Rxd3 15 Ke2 Rb3 (15...Rd8 16 g4 ±) 16 Bc3 Bc5 17 Nd2 is a complete failure for Black. Another source gives '12 0-0-0 Nb4' as the moves played but here too 13 a3! Nd3† 14 Bxd3 Rxd3 15 Kc2 Rd8 16 g4 Bc5 17 Nf3 is still comfortable for White. In both cases Black should try 12...Nf5 with play. It also seems that White can improve by 12 g4! Bc5 (12...Nd4 13 0-0-0) 13 Nf3 Nb4 (13...Nd4 14 Bg2!) 14 a3 Nd3† (14...Bxe3 15 axb4) 15 Bxd3 Rxd3 16 Ke2 Rhd8 (16...Rb3 17 Bc3 Bxe3 18 Kxe3 Bxc4 19 Nd2 + —) 17 Rhc1! threatens 18 f5 or 18 b4.

After 5 Nc3 the simplest equalizing method is 5...Bg4 6 Be2 (6 Qb3? Nc6 7 Qxb7 Nxd4 8 Bd3 Rb8 9 Qxa7 Ra8 10 Qb7 Ra5! threatens 11...Bc8 & 12...Nc6; 6 Nf3 e5! gives Black excellent play.) 6...Bxe2 7 Ngxe2 e6 8 0-0 Be7 9 Bf4 0-0 10 Qb3 Qc8 11 d5 Na6 = Kurajica — Bronstein, Brsac 1979. It seems that 5 Nc3 e5 is not at all clear and may actually favor White, but 5...Bg4! gives Black an easy game.

5 ....   g6

A plan based on 6...Bg4 and 6...e6 is inadequate here: 5...Bg4 6 Be2 e6 7 Be3 c6 8 0-0 Nbd7 9 Nc3 Be7 10 h3 Bh5 11 Ne5 Bxe2 12 Qxe2 Nxe5 13 dxe5 Nd7 14 Rad1 Qc7 15 f4 Vukovic — Popovic, Yugoslavia 1945. This position is discussed more fully in Chapter 3, A. note to Black's 6th move.

6 Nc3   Bg7

7 h3

A logical preventive move but not really necessary: 7 Be2 0-0 8 0-0 Bg4 (8...Nbd7 9 Bf4 c6 10 Qd2 Re8 11 Ne5 is clearly good for White, as is 8...c5 9 d5 e6 10 Be3 b6 11 Qb3 Re8 12 Rad1) 9 h3 (9 Be3!?) 9...Bxf3 10 Bxf3 Nc6 11 d5 Ne5 12 Be2 ±.

| 7 .... | 0-0 |
| 8 Be3 | Nbd7 |

8...c5 was a one-time only experiment seen in Bogolubov — K. Richter, Bad Nauheim 1935: 9 dxc5 Qa5 10 Qa4! Qxa4 11 Nxa4 Na6 12 a3 Bd7 13 Nc3 Rfc8 14 b4 b6 (14...Ne4 15 0-0-0!) 15 0-0-0! bxc5 16 b5 ±.

| 9 Qd2 | c6 |
| 10 Be2 | Rfe8 |

11 Rad1 Qa5 12 0-0 a6 13 a3 Qd8 11 Qc1 b6 15 Ne5 Bb7 16 c5! Qc7 17 Bf4 Qc8 18 Bc4 with a huge advantage for White in Tal — Bronstein, Moscow 1967. Black's play in this game was rather poor but it is clear that after 4...Nf6 Black has few chances of activity.

B3.

| 4 .... | Nb6 |

Diagram 44

After 4...Nb6

By putting pressure on White's pawn on c4 Black will be able to generate a certain amount of counterplay. Even so, with correct play by White, it is doubtful that Black will achieve equality.

B3a. 5 Nf3 g6; B3b. 5 Nf3 Bg4.

B3a.
5 Nf3

5 Nc3 is inaccurate as Black can play 5...e5! After 5...e5 White has: i. 6 d5; ii 6 Qe2; iii. 6 Be3. For 6 dxe5 see game # 11. For 6 Nf3 see game # 12.

i. 6 d5 c6! (6...Bc5 7 Ne4!? Be7 8 Nf3 Bg4 9 h3 Bxf3 10 Qxf3 0-0 followed by f7-f5; 6...Bb4!?) 7 Nf3 cxd5 8 cxd5 Bb4 9 Bb5† Bd7 10 Qb3 Bxc3† Hübner — Dzindzichashvili, Chicago 1982 was called a draw here which is a real surprise since 11 bxc3 Bxb5 12 Qxb5† Qd7 is quite good for Black!

ii. 6 Qe2!? Be7 (6...Qxd4 7 Nf3 Qd8!? has been suggested by Karaklaic)

76

7 dxe5 Nc6 8 Be3 Bf5 9 g4?! (9 Rd1) 9...Bg6 10 Rd1 Nb4! 11 Bxb6?
(11 Rxd8† Rxd8 12 Nd5 ∞) 11...axb6 12 Rxd8† Rxd8 13 Ne4 (13 Nd5
Nxd5 14 cxd5 Bb4† 15 Kd1 Rxd5† 16 Kc1 0-0! threatens 17...Rc5† &
18...Rd8† e.g. 17 Qe3 Rfd8! − +) 13...Rd4 14 Nd2 (14 Bg2 Nd3† 15 Kf1
Nf4 16 Qe1 Nxg2 17 Kxg2 Bxe4† 18 f3 Bc6 ∓; 14 f3? Bxe4 15 fxe4
Bh4†) 14...Nd3† 15 Kd1 Nxb2† 16 Kc1 Ba3 17 Nb1 (17 Ngf3 Na4† &
Nc3†) 17...Nd3† 18 Kc2 Nc1† 19 Kc3 Nxe2† 20 Bxe2 Bc5 Tarentjev −
Reshko, 1961.

iii. 6 Be3?! exd4 7 Bxd4 Nc6 8 Be3 Be6 9 c5 Nd7 10 Na4 Qh4 11 a3
0-0-0 ∓ Paoli − Commons, Lublin 1978.

5 ....   **g6**

6 h3

Interesting is 6 Bd2!? Bg7 7 Bc3 0-0 8 Be2 Bg4 9 0-0 Bxf3 10 Bxf3 Nc6
11 d5 Ne5 12 Be2 ± Mardle − Hollis, 1962. Allowing the pin by 6 Nc3 Bg4
is also quite reasonable: 7 Be2 Bg7 8 0-0 0-0 9 Be3 Nc6 10 d5 Bxf3 11
Bxf3 Ne5 12 c5! Nbc4 13 Bc1 Nxf3† (13...c6 Silman − Tidd, simultaneous
1982 when 14 Be2! cxd5 15 Qxd5 ±) 14 Qxf3 b6 15 Qe4 Nce5 16 c6!
The threat of 17 Bf4 gives White a large advantage.

6 ....   **Bg7**

7 Nc3

7 Be2 0-0 8 0-0 is inaccurate due to 8...c5! (8...Nc6 9 Be3 e5 10 d5 trans-
poses to note to White's 8th move, while 10 dxe5? Qxd1 11 Rxd1 Nxe5 12
Nxe5 Bxe5 13 Bd4 Nxc4 14 Bxc4 Rd8 15 Na3 Bxd4 16 Nb5 c5 Karanjac
− Maric, 1955 was a striking failure by White.) 9 d5 (9 dxc5? Qxd1 10 Rxd1
Na4) 9...e6 10 Bg5 Bf6 11 Qc1 exd5 12 cxd5 Bxg5 13 Nxg5 Qxd5 14 Nc3
Qe5 15 Re1 Nc6 16 Bf3 here the game Parma − Panno, 1966 was agreed
drawn, though after 16...Qg7 17 Nge4 (17 Nce4? h6; 17 Bxc6 bxc6 18 Nge4
c4) 17...c4 Black is doing quite well.

7 ....   **0-0**

7...Be6?! 8 Be3 Nxc4 (8...0-0 9 b3 c5 10 Rc1 ±) 9 Bxc4 Bxc4 10 Qa4†
b5 11 Nxb5 Bxb5 12 Qxb5† Nd7 13 Ne5 ±.

8 Be3

8 Be2 Nc6 9 Be3 e5 10 d5 Ne7 11 0-0 h6 (11...Nf5 12 Bg5 f6 13 Bc1
c5 14 Ne4 Qc7 15 b4! Nd6 16 Nxd6 Qxd6 17 bxc5 Qxc5 18 Qb3 Rd8 19
Be3 Qe7 20 Rfd1 e4 21 Nd4 Kh8 22 a4 f5 23 a5 Nd7 24 Ne6! was a disaster for Black. E. Kogan − B. Kogan, 1963.) 12 Qd2 Nf5 13 Rad1! (13 c5
Nxe3 14 fxe3 Nd7 15 b4 a5 16 a3 axb4 17 axb4 Rxa1 18 Rxa1 e4! 19
Nd4 Qh4 20 c6 bxc6 21 dxc6 Ne5 22 Rf1 Bxh3 23 gxh3 ½ - ½ Tal − Gur-
genidse, 1959.) 13...Nd7 14 c5! Nxe3 15 Qxe3 Re8 16 d6! c6 17 Bc4 Qa5
18 Ne4 b6? 19 Bxf7†! Kxf7 20 Qb3† Re6 21 Nfg5† hxg5 22 Nxg5† Kf6
23 h4! 1 - 0, Zieher − Stippekohl, West Germany 1977.

8 ....   **c5**

8...Nc6 9 Qd2 e5 10 d5 Ne7 11 g4 f5 12 0-0-0 fxg4 (for 12...Nd7 see game # 13) 13 Ng5 h6 14 Ne6 Bxe6 15 dxe6 Qxd2† 16 Rxd2 Nf5 17 c5! Nc8 18 hxg4 Nxe3 19 fxe3 Ne7 20 Rd7 + −, Shamkovich — Kusnetzov, USSR 1960.

9 d5

Other moves seem to allow equality:

i. 9 dxc5 Bxc3† 10 bxc3 Qxd1† 11 Rxd1 Na4;

ii. 9 Be2 cxd4 10 Nxd4 Nc6 11 Nxc6 Bxc3†! 12 bxc3 Qxd1† 13 Rxd1 bxc6 14 Bf3 Be6! 15 Bxc6 Rac8 16 Bd5 Bxd5 17 cxd5 Rxc3 18 0-0 Rd8 19 Bxb6 ½ - ½, Mokry — Hardicsay, Olomovc 1977.

9	Na6
10 Qd2	e5
11 0-0-0	f5
12 Bg5	

White stands better with 13 h4 (or d5-d6 if necessary) to follow.

B3b.

5 Nf3		Bg4

B3b1. 6 c5!; B3b2. 6 Be2.

B3b1.

6 c5!

Diagram 45   After 6 c5

This position clearly favors White. Aside from 6 c5 and 6 Be2, other moves offer nothing: 6 Be3 (for 6 Nc3 e5! see game # 12) 6...e5! 7 dxe5 (7 Be2 exd4 8 Nxd4 Bb4† =) 7...Qxd1† 8 Kxd1 Nc6 9 Be2 0-0-0† 10 Nbd2 Bxf3 11 gxf3 Nxe5 12 b3 Bb4 ∓ Boleslavski — Karaklaic, 1956.

6	N6d7!

First played in Zuidema — Karaklaic, Amsterdam 1965. The alternatives are unhealthy:

i. 6...Nd5 7 Qb3 Nc6 (7...b6?? 8 Ne5 1 - 0 Timman — Bakkali, Nice Olympiad 1974; 7...Bxf3 8 Qxb7! Ne3 9 Qxf3 Nc2† 10 Kd1 Nxa1 11 Qxa8 + −) 8 Qxb7 Ndb4 9 Bb5 Bd7 10 Bxc6 Nxc6 11 Qb3 Black does not have enough for the pawn.

ii. 6...Bxf3 7 Qxf3 Nd5 8 Qb3! b6 9 Bg5 Qd7 (9...h6 10 Bc4) 10 Nc3 e6 11 Nxd5 Qxd5 (11...exd5 12 c6! +—) 12 Qxd5 exd5 13 c6! Be7 14 Be3 Kd8 15 Rc1 Re8 16 g3! +—Suetin—Shamkovich, USSR 1964. If 16...Bg5 17 Kd2 Bxe3 18 fxe3 Re6 19 Bg2 Rd6 20 Rhf1 Ke7 21 Rf5.

7 Qb3

It is not clear what is best here. The quiet 7 Be2 e6 8 Qb3 b6 9 Be3 Be7 10 Nbd2 0-0 11 0-0 Nf6 only led to equality in Shamkovic — Rogoff, USA 1978. But both 7 Bg5 (see game # 14) and 7 Bc4 (see game # 15) give White excellent chances of obtaining an opening advantage.

7	Nc6
8 Be3	

8 d5 Bxf3 (8...Nxc5? 9 Qc4) 9 Qxf3 Nd4 (bad are 9...Nce5 10 Qc3 and 9...Nde5 10 Qb3! when neither 10...Nd4 11 Qa4† or 10...Na5 11 Qc3 are inspiring. Also bad is 9...Nb4 10 Qb3 a5 11 a3! Nxc5 [11...Na6 12 Bxa6! ±] 12 Qc3 Nba6 [12...Ne4 13 Bb5† c6 14 dxc6] 13 Bb5† leaves Black completely tied up.) 10 Qe4 e5! 11 dxe6 Nxe6 12 c6 Ndc5 (12...Nf6) gives Black an active game.

8	Bxf3
9 gxf3	Rb8

9...e5 should favor White after 10 Bc4! (10 d5 Na5 11 Qc3 c6 12 d6 is obviously good for White, but Black can do much better with 10...Nd4!) 10... Qf6 11 Bxf7† Qxf7 12 Qxb7 Rb8 13 Qxc6 exd4 (13...Rxb2 14 dxe5 ±) 14 Bxd4.

10 d5	Nce5
11 Be2	h5
12 Bd4!	c6
13 Qe3	

White stands better, e.g. 15...Qc7? 14 d6 Qa5† 15 Bc3 +—.

B3b2.

6 Be2	Nc6

6...c6 7 b3 g6?! 8 Ne5! Bxe2 9 Qxe2 Bg7 10 Bb2 N8d7 11 f4 ± Mardle — Cafferty, 1964; 6...e6 7 0-0 Be7 (7...Nc6 transposes to B2b2a.) 8 Ne5 Bxe2 9 Qxe2 Qxd4? 10 Rd1 Qc5 (10...Qh4 11 c5!) 11 b4! Qxb4 12 Ba3 Qa4 13 Bxe7 Kxe7 14 Nc3 Qe8 15 c5 N6d7 16 Nb5 Qc8 17 Rac1 Nxe5 18 Nd6! Qf8 19 Qxe5 Nd7 20 Nf5† Kd8 21 Qd4 1 - 0.

For 7...c5 see game # 16.

B3b2a. 7 0-0; B3b2b. 7 d5.

B3b2a.

7 0-0

(See diagram at top of next page)

Diagram 46   After 7 0-0

                    7 ....   e6

Move order for both sides becomes quite important in this line. For example in this position Black could try to equalize immediately by 7...Bxf3!? (instead of 7...e6) 8 Bxf3 Nxc4 9 Bxc6† (9 d5! N6e5 10 Be2 Nd6 is critical, when White has tons of play for the pawn i.e. 11 Qd4 Nd7 12 Re1! Nf6 13 Bg5.) 9...bxc6 10 Qa4 Nb6 11 Qxc6† Qd7. If White wishes to avoid this possibility he could use the following move order: 3 d4 Nxd5 4 Nf3 Bg4 5 Be2 e6 (or 5...Nc6) 6 0-0 Nc6 7 c4 Nb6 8 Nc3 going into the main line. If White does play the 4 c4 move order and Black wishes to avoid 7 d5 (B3b2b.) he can play 4...Nb6 5 Nf3 Bg4 6 Be2 e6 7 0-0 Nc6, etc.

                    8 Nc3!

i. 8 Be3 is inaccurate due to 8...Bxf3 9 Bxf3 Nxc4 10 Bxc6† bxc6 11 Qa4 Nb6 12 Qxc6† Qd7.

Diagram 47   After 12...Qd7

A very important position! After 13 Qxd7† Kxd7 J. Peters has said the following about the position: "If Black can exchange his bishop for White's knight, he gets the advantage. Thus 14 Rd1, 14 Re1, or 14 Nc3 are met by 14...Bb4!. White either weakens b3 (14 Rd1 Bb4 15 a3), accepts the isolated queen pawn (14 Rc1 Bb4 15 Nc3 Bxc3 16 Rxc3), or gets blockaded hanging pawns (14 Nc3 Bb4 15 Rac1 Bxc3 16 bxc3 Nc4 17 Rfd1 Kc6), or moves the knight twice (14 Nc3 Bb4 15 Ne4), not contesting d5."

Zapata — Dzindzichashvili, USA 1980 is a good example of Black's potential in endings of this sort: **13 Rc1 Qxc6 14 Rxc6 Kd7 15 Rc2 Bb4! 16 a3 Bd6 17 Nc3 Rhb8 18 Rac1 a5 19 Rd1 c6 20 Rdc1 Ra6 21 Bg5 a4 22 Bh4 Nd5 23 Nd1 f5 24 f3 Rb3 25 Bf2 Bf4 26 Ra1 g5 27 h3 h5 28 Kf1 h4** ∓.

Obviously not happy with this type of position, the game Rodriguez — Christiansen, Mexico 1978 saw White try for more with the sharp **10 Qb3!? Nb6 (10...Nd6 11 Bf4!) 11 d5 exd5 12 Bxb6 axb6 13 Bxd5 Qf6 14 Nc3 Be7 15 Ne4 Qg6 16 f4 0-0 17 f5 Qh6 18 f6 Bxf6 19 Nxf6† gxf6** & now **20 Bxc6 bxc6 21 Qg3† Kh8 22 Qxc7 Qe3† 23 Kh1** would have given White a slight edge.

ii. **8 b3 Bxf3 (8...Be7 9 Be3! 0-0 10 Nc3** ±, while **9 Bb2 0-0 10 Nbd2 f5** followed by **Bf6** gives Black good play.) **9 Bxf3 Nxd4 10 Bxb7 Rb8 11 Be3!** (**11 Be4 Be7** followed by **Bf6**) **11...c5! (11...Rxb7 12 Qxd4 Qxd4 13 Bxd4 c5 14 Be3 Be7 15 Nc3 0-0 16 Rad1 Rc8 17 Rd3 Kf8 18 Rfd1** gives White a small but lasting edge.) **12 Ba6! (12 Bxd4 Rxb7 13 Be3 Rd7** or **12 Be4 f5! 13 Bd3 Be7** both give White nothing) **12...Be7 13 Bxd4 Qxd4 14 Bb5† Kf8 15 Nd2 Bf6! (15...Rd8?! 16 Nf3 Qxd1 17 Raxd1 Rxd1 18 Rxd1 Bf6 19 a4!** leaves Black in real trouble) **16 Rc1 Rd8! (16...Ke7 17 Qe2** with **Ne4** or **Nf3** to follow. ±) After **16...Rd8** the position is equal.

8 ....   Bb4

8...Bxf3 9 Bxf3 Nxc4 10 d5! exd5 11 Re1† Be7 12 Nxd5 Nd6 13 Bf4 ± J. Whitehead — Peters, USA 1978. Instead of **9...Nxc4** Black might try **9... Nxd4**, but after **10 Bxb7 Rb8 11 Ba6 Be7** White gains a significant advantage with either **12 Nb5** or **12 Be3 Nf5 13 Bb5† Kf8 14 Qf3 Nxe3 15 fxe3** Biyiases — Green, Canada 1978.

8...Be7!? 9 b3 0-0 10 Be3 ± since **10...Bf6** can always be met by **11 Ne4!** Also possible is **9 Be3 Bxf3 10 Bxf3 Nxc4 11 Bxc6† bxc6 12 Qa4 Nb6 13 Qxc6† Qd7 14 Qf3** the point is that White has gotten the useful **Nc3** in, while Black has played the inferior **Be7** (instead of **Bb4**. See note to White's 8th move for detailed discussion). Due to this, White won't be forced into weakening his b3 square (by a2-a3), therefore giving Black far less counterplay than he usually gets. It is unclear, however, if White can gain any real advantage from all of this. For a good example of the chances available to White, see game # 17.

It should be mentioned that after **8...Be7**, the sharp **9 d5** seems a bit premature: **9 d5 exd5 10 cxd5 Nb4 11 h3 Bh5 12 Qb3 0-0 13 Rd1 a5! 14 Rd2 a4 15 Qd1 Ra5.** Uusi — Eller, 1958. White's aggression has backfired.

9 d5   Ne7

9...exd5? 10 cxd5 Ne7 11 Qd4 ±.

10 h3

Also very strong is **10 Qb3 a5 11 Rd1.**

10 dxe6?! Bxe6 11 Qb3 Nc6 12 Rd1 Qc8 13 Nd5?! (13 Bf4) 13...Bd6

14 Qc3 0-0 15 b3 f6 16 Ne3 Nd7 17 Bb2 a5 18 a3 Nc5 19 Nd5 Qe8 20 Re1 Qf7 led to a fine game for Black. Taulbut — Peters, Hastings 1978/79.

10	Bxf3
11 Bxf3	exd5
12 cxd5	±.

12...Bxc3 13 bxc3 Nbxd5 14 c4 regains the pawn, while 14 Ba3! seems crushing.

B3b2b.

7 d5

A critical move, though it can be avoided by Black. (See note to 7...e6, B2b2a., right after Diagram 46.

7	Bxf3
8 Bxf3	Ne5
9 b3!	

9 Be2 c6! 10 Qd4 Ng6 11 0-0 e5! 12 Qe4 cxd5 13 cxd5 Qxd5 14 Nc3 Qxe4 15 Nxe4 Be7 is known to be good for Black, Kuprejanov — Karaklaic, Yugoslavia 1962. But 14 Qxd5! Nxd5 15 Bb5† gives White play: 15...Ke7 16 Rd1 Rd8 (16...Ke6?? 17 Bc4 Rd8 18 Nc3 Nge7 19 Be3 + −; 16...Nf6 17 Bg5 a6 18 Ba4 b5 19 Bb3 with Nc3 to follow gives a lot of pressure) 17 Bc4 Nb4! 18 Rxd8 Kxd8 19 Nc3 Ke8! 20 Be3 Nc2 21 Rd1 Nxe3 22 fxe3 White has full compensation.

9	c6

9...g6 is worse: 10 Bb2 Bg7 11 Nc3 c6? 12 0-0 Nxf3† 13 Qxf3 cxd5 14 c5! Spielmann — Mieses, Mannheim 1914. After 14...Nc8 15 Rad1 e6 16 Nxd5! Bxb2 17 Nb6 is winning for White.

10 dxc6

10 Nc3 Nxf3† 11 Qxf3 cxd5 12 cxd5 g6 13 Bd2 Bg7 gives White nothing, while the sharper 12 c5 Nd7 13 Qxd5 Qa5 14 Bd2 e6 (14...Qxc5 =; 14...Rd8?? 15 c6! Qxd5 16 Nxd5 wins; 14...0-0-0?! 15 Ne4! Qa6 16 Qxf7!) 15 Qxb7 Rb8 16 Qc6 Qxc5 = .

10	Qxd1†
11 Bxd1	Nd3†

11...Nxc6 12 Bb2 ±.

12 Kd2	0-0-0!?

12...Nxf2 13 cxb7! Rd8† 14 Kc2 Nxh1 15 Bf4 Nd7 16 Bc7 e6 17 Bf3 Sabkov — Nenzev, 1967. White is winning. 12...Rd8 13 cxb7! is the same.

13 cxb7†	Kb8!

13...Kxb7 14 Ke2.

14 Kc2

14 Bf3!? Nxf2† 15 Kc2 (15 Ke2? Nxh1 16 Bf4† e5 17 Bxe5† Bd6 18 Bxd6† Rxd6 19 c5 Re6†) 15...Nxh1 16 Bf4† e5 17 Bxe5† Bd6 18 Bxd6† Rxd6 19 c5 Rd7 (19...Rh6!?; 19...Re6? 20 cxb6 axb6? 21 Nc3 + −) 20 cxb6 axb6 21 Nc3 Nf2 the position is obscure.

14 ....   **g5!**

Many interesting possibilities:

i. 14...g6 15 Be2 Nb4† 16 Kb2 Bg7† 17 Nc3 Nd3† (17...Rd3!?) 18 Bxd3 Rxd3 19 Bf4† Kxb7 20 Rac1.

ii. 14...Nb4† 15 Kc3 g6? (15...a5 16 a3 g6 17 axb4 Bg7† 18 Kc2 Bxa1 19 bxa5) 16 Bf4† Kxb7 17 Bf3† Kc8 18 Kxb4 (18 Be5) e5† (18...Bg7 19 Nd2 winning, and not 19 Nc3 a5†) 19 Kb5 + −. Best after 14...Nb4† is 15 Kc3 Nd3! when 16 Be2 g6 transposes into i., while 16...g5 transposes into the main line (14...g5).

iii. 14...e5 15 Be3 f5.

15 Bd2

15 Nc3 Nb4† 16 Kb1 Bg7 17 Bb2 Rd2; 15 Be2 Nb4† (15...Bg7 16 Bxd3 Bxa1 17 Bxg5 f6 18 Be3 Bd4 19 Be4 or 18...Kxb7 19 Be4† Kb8 20 Nc3 both are good for White.) 16 Kb2 (16 Kc3 a5!) 16...Bg7† 17 Nc3 Nd3† 18 Kc2 (18 Bxd3 Rxd3 − +, White no longer has the saving move Bf4†) 18... Nb4† =.

15 ....   **Bg7**

Black wants to trade bishops. Possible is 15...Nxf2 16 Rf1 (16 Bc3? Nxh1 17 Bxh8 f6 traps the bishop) 16...Nxd1 17 Rxd1 Bg7 18 Nc3! h6 (18... Bxc3!? 19 Bxc3 f6) 19 c5 Nd7 and now 20 Be3 (20 c6 Ne5 gives White nothing) followed by a queenside push should be good for White.

16 Bc3	**Bxc3**
17 Nxc3	**Nxf2**
18 Rf1	**Nxd1**
19 Raxd1	**f6**
20 c5	**Nd7**
21 b4!	

21 c6 Ne5 =.

21 ....   **Kxb7**

A tough endgame that is favorable to White.

Chapter Four

1 e4	d5
2 exd5	Nf6
3 Nc3	

Diagram 48   After 3 Nc3

This position also comes about by the following sequence in the Alekhine's Defense: 1 e4 Nf6 2 Nc3 d5 3 exd5. This variation is not very dangerous and I will give only a few lines to demonstrate this.

3	Nxd5
4 Bc4	

4 Be2? e5 5 Bf3 Be6 6 Nge2 Nc6 7 d3 Bc5 8 Ne4 Be7 9 c3 0-0 10 Qc2 f5 ∓ ;

4 d4 Bf5 = ;

4 Qf3 Nb6 prevents White from playing Bc4.

4	Nb6

Many good alternatives here:

4...Nxc3; 4...Be6!?; 4...c6; 4...e6.

An example of 4...e6 is 5 Nf3 Be7 6 0-0 0-0 7 d4 b6 8 Ne4 Bb7 9 Qe2 Nd7 10 Rd1 c5 11 dxc5 Nxc5 equal, according to Hort.

5 Bb3	Nc6!
6 Nf3	e5
7 d3	Be7
8 h3	0-0

= .

Illustrative Games, Part Two

Game # 1
Zentai — Dr. Tiszay, correspondence 1951

1 e4 d5 2 exd5 Nf6 3 c4 c6 4 dxc6 Nxc6 5 Nf3 e5 6 Nc3? e4 7 Ng5 Bf5
8 f3 Bc5 9 fxe4 0-0!

Diagram 49   After 9...0-0

10 d3

10 exf5 Re8† 11 Be2 (11 Ne2 Qd4 12 Nh3 Ne5! 13 d3 Bb4† wins)
11...Qd4 12 Nh3 (12 Qa4 Qf2† 13 Kd1 Qxg2 14 Bf3 Qxg5 15 d4 Qxf5
— +, or 12 Rf1 Qh4† 13 g3 Qxh2 with a winning attack.) 12...Qh4†
(Schwarz' 12...Re5 13 Rf1 Nb4 14 Rf3 Qh4† 15 Kf1 Ng4 16 d4 Nxh2†
17 Kg1 Nxf3† is also strong.) 13 Kf1 Re5 14 Bf3 Rae8 Black should score a
quick win.

10...Re8 11 Bf4 h6 12 Nf3 Ng4 13 Bg3 Nb4 14 Nd5 Bxe4! 15 dxe4 Rxe4†
16 Be2 Qa5 17 Nc3 Rd8 18 Qa4 Nd3† 19 Kf1 Ne3† 20 Kg1 Nxc4† 21 Kf1
Ne3† 22 Kg1 Rxa4 White resigns.

Game # 2
Soultanbeieff — Jerolim, 1954

1 e4 d5 2 exd5 Nf6 3 c4 c6 4 dxc6 Nxc6 5 Nf3 e5 6 d3 Bf5 7 Bg5

7 Be2 Bb4† 8 Bd2 (8 Nc3? e4! 9 dxe4 Qxd1† 10 Bxd1 Nxe4 11 Bd2
Nxd2 12 Kxd2 0-0-0† 13 Kc1 Bxc3 14 bxc3 Rhe8 Black has a wonderful
position) 8...Bxd3 9 Bxb4 Nxb4 10 Qa4† Nc6 11 Nxe5 (11 Nc3!?) 11...
Bxe2 12 Nxc6 Qd7 13 Kxe2 and now 13...0-0 is recommended by Schwarz
but 14 Rd1 seems safe for White.

7...Bb4† 8 Nc3 Qd7! 9 Bxf6 gxf6 10 Nh4 0-0-0 11 Nxf5 Qxf5 12 Be2
Rhg8 13 0-0 Kb8 14 Nd5 Rg7 15 a3?!

15 Kh1.

15...Rdg8 16 g3 Bc5 17 Bf3? Rxg3† 18 hxg3 Rxg3† 19 Bg2 Qh3 20 Qf3
Nd4! White resigned.

This game is not very convincing and Black would be well advised to try
6...Bc5 or 6...e4!, both of which give Black all the chances.

Game # 3

Tereschtschenko — Beschan, correspondence 1963

1 e4 d5 2 exd5 Nf6 3 c4 c6 4 dxc6 Nxc6 5 Nf3 e5 6 d3 Bc5 7 Be2 Ng4
8 0-0 Qb6! 9 Qe1 Nb4

Crude but effective.

10 Na3 Bf5

(Diagram →)

11 d4

11 h3

11...exd4 12 Nxd4 Nxf2! 13 Bf3†
Kf8 14 Be3 Nfd3 15 Qc3 Bg6 16
Kh1 Re8 17 Bg1 a6 18 h3 h5 19 b3
Rh6 20 Bd5 Re5 21 Nf3 Re2 22
Bxc5 Qxc5 23 Qd4 Qe7 24 Nh4
Nxd5 25 Nxg6† Rxg6 26 Qxd3 Rgxg2 0 - 1

Game # 4

Maroczy — Helling, Dresden 1936

1 e4 d5 2 exd5 Nf6 3 Bb5† c6 4 dxc6 bxc6 5 Be2 e5 6 d3 Bc5 7 Nf3 Ng4
8 0-0 f5 9 Nc3 Qf6 10 Qe1! 0-0 11
h3 h5 12 hxg4 hxg4 13 Ng5 g3 14
Na4 Bxf2† 15 Rxf2 f4 16 Ne4 Qh4

(Diagram →)

17 Nxg3! fxg3 18 Rxf8† Kxf8 19 Bf3!
Nd7

19...Qxa4 20 Qxe5 leaves White
firmly in control.

20 Qe4 Qh2† 21 Kf1 Nf6 22 Qxc6 e4
23 dxe4 Qh1† 24 Ke2 Ba6†

24...Rb8 25 Qd6†

25 Qxa6 Rd8 26 Bf4! Qxa1 27 Bd6† Kf7 28 Qc4† Kg6 29 e5 Qg1 30 Qc5
Qc1 31 exf6 gxf6 32 Be4† Kh6 33 Qf5 1 - 0

Game # 5

DeRiviere — Dubois, Paris 1858

1 e4 d5 2 exd5 Nf6 3 Bb5† Bd7
4 Bxd7†?! Qxd7 5 c4 c6 6 dxc6 Nxc6
7 Nf3 e5 8 0-0 e4!? 9 Re1 0-0-0! 10
Ng5 Qf5! 11 Nxf7 Bc5! 12 Rf1 Ng4!
13 Nxh8 Nxf2 (Diagram →)
14 Qe1 (14 Rxf2 Qxf2† 15 Kh1 e3!
wins; 14 d4!? exd3 15 Qe1 Nb4!)
14...Rf8 15 d4! Bxd4 16 Nd2
(16 Be3? Bxe3 17 Qxe3 Nh3†)

16...Nd3† 17 Kh1 Nxe1 18 Rxf5 Rxf5 19 h3 e3 20 Ne4 Rf1† 21 Kh2 Be5† 22 g3 Nd4 23 h4 h5 24 Ng5 Nef3† 25 Nxf3 Rf2† 26 Kh3 Nxf3 0 - 1

Game # 6
Pribyl — Gipslis, Tallinn 1977

1 e4 d5 2 exd5 Nf6 3 Bb5† Bd7 4 Be2 Nxd5 5 d4 Bf5 6 Nf3 e6 7 a3 Be7 8 c4 Nb6 9 Nc3 0-0 10 Be3 Nc6 11 0-0 Bf6 12 b3 Qd7 13 Ra2 Rad8 14 Rd2 Qe7 15 Qc1 Rd7 16 Rfd1 Rfd8 17 h3 h6 18 b4 Bg6 19 Qb2 Qf8 20 Qb3 Kh7 21 Kh1 Kh8 22 Bf1 Bh5 23 g4 Bg6 24 h4 e5 (Diagram →)

25 d5 Nd4 26 Nxd4 exd4 27 Bxd4 Bxh4 28 f4 Kg8 29 f5 Bh7 30 Ne4 Nc8 31 Nc5 Nd6 32 Nxd7 Rxd7 33 Qf3 Re7 34 Bd3 Qe8 35 Re2 Qa4 36 Rxe7 Bxe7 37 c5 Nb5 38 Bxb5 Qxb5 39 Re1 Bf8 40 f6 g5 41 Be5 a5 42 d6 cxd6 43 Bxd6 axb4 44 axb4 Bg6 45 Bxf8 Kxf8 46 Qh3 Qc6† 47 Kg1 1 - 0

Game #7
R. Fischer — Bergraser, Monte Carlo 1967

1 e4 d5 2 exd5 Nf6 3 Bb5† Bd7 4 Bc4 Bg4 5 f3 Bf5 6 g4 Bc8 7 Nc3 Nbd7 8 g5 Nb6 9 Bb5† Nfd7 10 f4! Nxd5 11 Nxd5 c6 12 Bc4 cxd5 13 Bxd5
(Diagram →)

13...Ne5 (13...e5 14 Nf3 Qa5 15 Bb3 [15 c4!?; 15 Bc4!?] 15...e4 16 Qe2 Nc5 with compensation, according to O'Kelly. Untested, unproved.) 14 Be4 Bg4 15 Nf3 Nc6 16 d4! e6 (16...Bxf3 17 Bxf3 Nxd4 18 Bxb7) 17 c3 Qc7 18 Qa4 f6 19 Rg1 Bxf3 20 Bxf3 0-0-0 21 Qc4 Kb8! 22 Be3! Bd6 23 gxf6 gxf6 24 Bxc6 bxc6 25 Rf1 e5 26 fxe5 fxe5 27 0-0-0 Rhf8 28 Rxf8 Rxf8 29 dxe5 Bxe5? 30 Qb4† 1 - 0

Game # 8
Lombardy — Gaprindashvili, Lone Pine 1977

1 e4 d5 2 exd5 Nf6 3 d4 Nxd5 4 Nf3 Bf5 5 c3 e6 6 Qb3 Qc8 (6...Nb6 7 a4! ±) 7 Nh4! Bg6 8 Nxg6 hxg6 9 g3 Be7 10 Bg2 0-0
(See diagram at top of next page)

11 0-0!
(11 Bxd5 exd5 12 Qxd5 c5 13 dxc5 Bxc5 14 0-0 Rd8 gives Black counter-

Diagram 55
Lombardy — Gaprindashvili
After 10...0-0

play.)
**11...c6 12 c4 Nf6 13 Nc3 Nbd7 14
Bf4 Nh5 15 Be3 e5?! 16 d5 Nhf6
17 Rad1 Nc5 18 Qa3 cxd5 19 Nxd5
Nxd5 20 Rxd5 b6 21 Rxe5 Bf6
22 Bxc5 1 - 0**

Game # 9
Nedelkovic — Kozomara, Belgrade 1960

**1 e4 d5 2 exd5 Nf6 3 d4 Nxd5 4
Nf3 Bg4 5 Be2 e6 6 c3 Nd7 7 h3
Bh5 8 Qb3 Bd6! 9 Qxb7 0-0 10
0-0 Rb8 11 Qa6 Rb6**

(Diagram →)

12 Qc4
12 Qd3? Bg6 13 Qd1 Bxb1 14 Rxb1
Nxc3
**12...Qa8 13 Ne5? Bxe5 14 Bxh5 Bf4
15 Bxf4 Nxf4 16 Bf3 Qd8 17 b4 e5!
18 Rd1 Qg5 19 Kf1 e4! 20 Bxe4 Re8
21 Bf3 Rg6 22 g3 Qf5 23 g4 Nxh3! 0 - 1**

Game # 10
Schroter — Ludwig, correspondence 1932

**1 e4 d5 2 exd5 Nf6 3 d4 Nxd5 4
c4 Nb4 5 Qa4† N8c6 6 d5? b5!**

(Diagram →)

7 cxb5 (7 Qxb5 Nc2† 8 Kd2 [8 Kd1
Bd7! 9 dxc6 Bg4† 10 Kxc2 Qd1†]
8...Bd7! 9 dxc6 Bf5† 10 Qd5 Nb4
11 Qxd8† Rxd8† 12 Kc3 Nc2 13
Bf4 e5! 14 Bxe5 Bb4† 15 Kb3 Rb8
16 Bxc7 0-0 17 Bxb8 Rxb8 18 a3
Bxa3† 19 Kc3 Bb4† 20 Kb3 Bd2†
21 Ka4 [21 Ka2 Bc1!] 21...Rb4†

22 Ka5 Nd4! 0 - 1 Rhode — Zitzewitz, correspondence 1910; 7 Qd1 Nd4
8 Na3 e5 9 Ne2 Bf5 etc.) 7...Nd4 8 Na3 e5 9 dxe6 (9 Bd2 Nxd5 10 Ne2
Nb6 11 Qd1 Bg4 12 Bc3 Bc5 13 Bxd4 exd4 14 Qb3 c3. Middleton — Lotfi
correspondence 1956.) 9...Bxe6 10 Be3 (10 Bd2 Qd5! 11 Bxb4 Bxb4† 12

12 Qxb4 Qe4† 13 Ne2 Nf3† 14 gxf3 Qxb4† 15 Nc3 Qxb2 − +) 10...Qh4!
11 b6† (11 0-0-0 Ne2† 12 Kd2 Nxg1 13 Rxg1 0-0-0†) 11...c6 12 b7 Rd8
13 Rd1 Bc5 14 Ne2? (14 Bxd4 is better) 14...Bb3! 15 Rxd4 Bxa4 16 b8(Q)
Bxd4! 17 Qb7 Nd3† 18 Kd2 Bxe3† 0 - 1

Game # 11
Padevski − Karaklaic, Ljubljana 1955
1 e4 d5 2 exd5 Nf6 3 d4 Nxd5 4 c4 Nb6 5 Nc3 e5 6 dxe5 Qxd1† 7 Nxd1
7 Kxd1 Nc6 8 f4 Bg4† 9 Ke1 Nb4 10 Kf2 0-0-0 11 a3 Nd3† 12 Kg3 Bf5
13 Nf3 Bc5 14 Bxd3 Rxd3 15 Re1 Nxc4 with a large advantage, Belinkov −
Gik, USSR 1963.) 7...Nc6 8 f4

(Diagram →)

8...Be6 (Other moves also give Black
good chances: i. 8...Nb4 9 Ne3 Bc5
10 a3 Nc6 11 b4?! Bd4 12 Ra2 Be6
13 Rc2 0-0 14 Bd3 Rad8 15 Ke2?
Bxe3 16 Kxe3? Rxd3† 17 Kxd3
Bf5† 18 Kc3 Na4† 19 Kb3 Nd4†
20 Kxa4 Bxc2† 0 - 1 Mogordosiev −
Kusnetzov, USSR 1963; ii. 8...f6 9
exf6 Bb4† 10 Kf2 [10 Bd2 0-0!]
10...gxf6 11 Be3 Be6 12 Rc1 0-0-0 ∓ Rubinstein − Walter, Mährisch Ostrau
1923; iii. 8...Bb4† 9 Kf2 Be6 10 b3 0-0-0 has been recommended by Panov.)
9 Ne3 (9 b3 0-0-0 10 Nf3 [10 Ne3 Bc5 11 a3 Rhe8] 10...Bc5 11 Ne3 Nb4
12 a3 [12 Kf2? Nc2 13 Rb1 Rd1 14 Ke2 Nxe3] 12...Nd3† 13 Bxd3 Rxd3
14 f5 Bd7 15 Nd5 Nxd5 16 cxd5 Bxf5 White is crushed.) 9...Bc5 10 b3
0-0-0 11 Nf3 Nb4 12 a3? (12 Ke2 Nd3 13 g3 f6 is a better defense though
still good for Black.) 12...Nd3† 13 Ke2 Nxf4† 14 Kf2 Nd3† 15 Bxd3 Rxd3
16 Rb1 Rhe8 17 Ke2 Rdd8 18 Bb2 a5 19 a4 Bxe3 20 Kxe3 Bf5 21 Rbc1
Rd3† 22 Kf4 Rxb3 23 Bc3 Nxa4 24 Bxa5 Be6 25 Nd4 Rd3 26 Nb5 Nc5
27 Nxc7 g5† 28 Kxg5 Rg8† 29 Kh6 Rg6† 30 Kxh7 Bf5 31 h4 Rdg3 0 - 1

Game # 12
Emanuel Lasker − Alekhine, St Petersburg 1914
1 e4 d5 2 exd5 Nf6 3 d4 Nxd5 4 c4 Nb6 5 Nc3 e5 6 Nf3 Bg4 7 c5
(7 Be2 Bxf3 8 Bxf3 exd4 9 0-0 [9 Qe2† is inferior due to 9...Be7 10 c5
dxc3 11 Bxb7 N8d7 12 cxb6 Rb8 13 Bxf3 Rxb6. Braun − Honfi, correspondence 1957] 9...dxc3 10 Re1† Be7 11 Bg5 f6 12 Bh5† g6 13 Bxf6 0-0
14 Bxe7 Qxd1 15 Bxd1 cxb2 16 Rb1 Re8 17 Bb3 Nc6 18 Bf6 Na5 = Puc −
Karaklaic, 1951) 7...exd4 (7...N6d7! is good for Black.) 8 Ne4! N6d7 9
Qxa4 Qe7 10 Bb5 Nc6 (10...c6 11 0-0! cxb5 12 Nd6†) 11 Bxc6 bxc6 12
0-0 Bxf3 13 gxf3 0-0-0 14 Qa4 Ne5! 15 Kg2 Qe6! 16 Qxa7 Qf5 17 Qa8†
Kd7 18 Rd1† Ke6 19 Qxd8 Qxf3† 20 Kg1 Be7! 21 Qd4 Qg4† 22 Kh1
Qf3† 23 Kg1 Qg4† ½ - ½

Game # 13
Zhuravlev — Shamkov, USSR 1980

1 e4 d5 2 exd5 Nf6 3 d4 Nxd5 4 c4 Nb6 5 Nf3 g6 6 h3 Bg7 7 Nc3 0-0 8
Be3 Nc6 9 Qd2 e5 10 d5 Ne7 11 g4!
f5 12 0-0-0 (Diagram →)

12...Nd7 (12...e4 13 Ng5 h6 14 Ne6
Bxe6 15 dxe6 Qxd2 16 Rxd2 Bxc3
17 bxc3 f4 18 Bc5 Rfe8 19 Re2 or
19 Rd7 ± ; 12...fxg4 13 Ng5 Nf5 14
hxg4 Nxe3 15 Qxe3 Bg4 16 Rxh7!)
13 Bh6 a6 (13...fxg4 14 hxg4! Rxf3
15 Bxg7 Kxg7 16 Qh6†) 14 Bxg7
Kxg7 15 Qe3! ± e4 16 Ng5 Nf6
17 Ne6 Bxe6 18 dxe6 Qe8 19 g5!
Nh5 20 Rd7 Kg8 21 c5! Rc8 22 Bc4 b5 23 Bb3 c6 24 Rhd1 b4 25 Ne2 f4
26 Qxe4 Rf5 27 h4 Rxc5† 28 Kb1 Qf8 29 Rxe7! Qxe7 30 Rd7 Qe8 31
e7† Kh8 32 Qd4† Kg7 33 Rd8 1 - 0

Game # 14
Varlamov — Shulman, Leningrad 1979

1 e4 d5 2 exd5 Nf6 3 d4 Nxd5 4 Nf3 Bg4 5 c4 Nb6 6 c5 N6d7 7 Bg5 Nf6
(7...g6 8 h3 Bxf3 9 Qxf3 c6 [9...Nc6 10 Bc4! Nf6 11 Bb5 Qd5 12 Bxf6
Qxf3 13 gxf3 gxf6 14 d5 wins a piece] 10 Bc4 Nf6 11 Qb3! Black's game
was disintegrating in Kudinov — Neuholf, correspondence 1975-76; perhaps
7...h6!? 8 Bg3 g5 is possible, though Black should avoid 7...h6 8 Bh4 b6?
9 Bc4! g5 10 Bxg5! hxg5 11 Nxg5
Be6 12 Bxe6 fxe6 13 Qf3 which wins
for White.) 8 Nbd2 Nbd7 9 Qb3 Qc8
10 Bc4 e6 11 0-0 Be7 12 Ne5 Bf5
13 f4 h6 14 Bh4 Ne4 15 Nxe4 Nxe5
(15...Bxh4 16 Ng3 ±) 16 fxe5 Bxh4
17 Rxf5! exf5 18 Bxf7† Ke7 19 Nd6!
(Diagram →)

19...cxd6 20 cxd6† Kd8 21 e6 Rf8
22 Re1! Bxe1 23 e7† Kd7 24 Qe6†
Kc6 25 d7† 1 - 0

Game # 15
Christiansen — Commons, USA 1978

1 e4 d5 2 exd5 Nf6 3 d4 Nxd5 4 Nf3 Bg4 5 c4 Nb6 6 c5 N6d7 7 Bc4 e6
8 Be3 (Byrne — Rogoff, USA Championship 1978, went 8 h3 Bh5 9 Be3 Nc6
10 Nc3 Be7 11 a3! e5 12 d5 Nd4 13 g4! Nxf3† 14 Qxf3 Bg6 15 b4 0-0
16 Rd1 ± but Black should play 9...b6 when 10 Nc3 bxc5 11 d5 e5 12 d6
no longer works since f7 is now guarded by the bishop on h5.) 8...b6 9 Nc3
bxc5? (9...c6 10 b4 a5 11 a3 axb4 12 axb4 Rxa1 13 Qxa1 bxc5 14 bxc5

Bxf3 15 gxf3 is a better choice but
also seems to be favorable to White,
e.g. 15...e5? 16 Ne4! f5 17 Ng5 f4
18 Bf7† Ke7 19 Qa2.)

(Diagram →)

10 d5! ± Bd6 (10...e5 11 d6!
Bxd6? 12 Bxf7† Kxf7 13 Qd5†)
11 dxe6 fxe6? (11...Bxe6 12 Bxe6
fxe6 13 Ng5 Qf6 14 Qb3 ±)
12 h3 Bf5 13 g4 Bg6 14 Bxe6 Nc6
15 0-0 h6 16 Qa4! Nb4 17 Rfe1
Nd3 18 Bxd7† Qxd7 19 Bg5† Be5 20 Nxe5 Qxa4 21 Nxd3† Kf8 22 Be7†
Kg8 23 Nxa4 Bxd3 24 Nxc5   1 - 0

Game # 16
Schaposchnikov — Redeleit, correspondence 1960
1 e4 d5 2 exd5 Nf6 3 d4 Nxd5 4 c4 Nb6 5 Nf3 Bg4 6 Be2 e6 7 0-0 c5 8
d5! exd5 9 cxd5 Qxd5 10 Qe1 Qe6 11 Nc3 Be7 12 Ng5 Bxg5 13 Bxg4
Qxe1 14 Rxe1† Be7 15 Nb5 Na6 16 Bg5 f6 17 Bf4 Kf7 18 Rxe7†! Kxf7
19 Re1† Kd8 20 Nd6 Kc7 21 Nf5† Kc6 22 Bf3† Kb5 23 Nd6† Ka5 24
Nxb7† Kb5 25 Nd6† Ka5 26 Bd2†   1 - 0

Game # 17
Ostermeyer — Strauss, London 1980
1 e4 d5 2 exd5 Nf6 3 d4 Nxd5 4 Nf3 Bg4 5 Be2 e6 6 0-0 Nc6 7 h3 Bh5
8 c4 Nb6 9 Nc3 Be7 10 Be3 Bxf3 11 Bxf3 Nxc4 12 Bxc6† bxc6 13 Qa4
Nb6 14 Qxc6† Qd7 15 Qf3 0-0 16 Rac1 a5 17 Rc2 a4 18 Rfc1 Rfb8 19
Bf4 Bd6 20 Be5! Ra5? (20...f6) 21 Qg3 f6 22 Ne4! Qf7 23 Bxd6 cxd6
24 Nxd6 Qf8 25 Rc6 Raa8 26 Qe3 Qe7 27 Nf5   1 - 0

Index

Illustrative Games, Part Two

References Consulted

Skandinavisch und Jugoslavisch by Rolf Schwarz

Encyclopedia of Chess Openings

Chess Openings Illustrated: The Center Counter by J. DuMont

Chess Archives

Modern Chess Theory

Skandinavisk by Fries Nielsen

About The Authors

John Grefe is an International Master who received his title in 1975. In 1973, he and Grandmaster Lubosh Kavalek shared first place in the U. S. Closed Championship. Winner of numerous Swiss events, including the 1980 American Open, Grefe currently shares the title of Northern California state champion, an honor he won outright last year. His current rating of 2550 makes him approximately the fifteenth highest ranked player in the United States. He is also the author of *The Best of Lone Pine,* published by RHM Press, and *The 35 Best Chess Books,* from Players Press.

Jeremy Silman, a chess professional since 1974, is a U. S. Senior Master. His rating, which floats around 2550, makes him one of the strongest (if not the strongest) untitled players in the United States. Mr. Silman, one of the most successful tournament players in Northern California, tied for first in the 1981 U. S. Open, and currently shares the title of Northern California State Champion with Grefe and C. Powell.